MW00978994

THEODORE
ROOSEVELT

THEODORE ROOSEVELT

Book Editors:

TOM LANSFORD, PH.D.
UNIVERSITY OF SOUTHERN MISSISSIPPI

ROBERT P. WATSON, PH.D.
FLORIDA ATLANTIC UNIVERSITY

DANIEL LEONE, *President*
BONNIE SZUMSKI, *Publisher*
SCOTT BARBOUR, *Managing Editor*
SANDRA SOMERS, *Series Editor*

San Diego • Detroit • New York • San Francisco • Cleveland
New Haven, Conn. • Waterville, Maine • London • Munich

973.911 Theodore

Theodore Roosevelt

T0054463

LIBRARY OF CONGRESS CATALOGING-IN-PUBLICATION DATA

Theodore Roosevelt / Tom Lansford and Robert P. Watson, book editors.
    p. cm. — (Presidents and their decisions)
Includes bibliographical references and index.
ISBN 0-7377-1408-5 (lib. bdg. : alk. paper) —
ISBN 0-7377-1409-3 (pbk. : alk. paper)
    1. Roosevelt, Theodore, 1858–1919. 2. United States—Politics and government—1901–1909. 3. United States—Politics and government—1901–1909—Decision making. 4. Presidents—United States—Biography.
I. Lansford, Tom. II. Watson, Robert P., 1962– . III. Series.
E756 .T44 2003
973.91'1'092—dc21   2002073213

Printed in the United States of America

Contents

CHAPTER 4: THE GREAT WHITE FLEET AND U.S. NAVAL POWER

FOREWORD

"THE PRESIDENCY OF THE UNITED STATES IS OFTEN DE-
scribed as the most powerful office in the world,"
writes Forrest McDonald in *The American Presidency: An
Intellectual History*. "In one sense this description is accurate," he says, "for even casual decisions made in the White
House can affect the lives of millions of people." But Mc-
Donald also notes that presidential power "is restrained by
the countervailing power of Congress, the courts, the bureaucracy, popular opinion, the news media, and state and
local governments. What presidents do have is awesome
responsibilities combined with unique opportunities to
persuade others to do their bidding—opportunities enhanced by the possibility of dispensing favors, by the mystique of presidential power, and by the aura of monarchy
that surrounds the president."

The way various presidents have used the complex
power of their office is the subject of Greenhaven Press's
Presidents and Their Decisions series. Each volume in the
series examines one particular president and the key decisions he made while in office.

Some presidential decisions have been made in a relatively brief period of time, as with Abraham Lincoln's sus-
pension of the writ of habeus corpus at the start of the
Civil War. Others were refined as they were implemented
over a period of years, as was the case with Franklin De-
lano Roosevelt's struggle to lead the country out of the
Great Depression. Some presidential actions are generally
lauded by historians—for example, Lyndon Johnson's support of the civil rights movement in the 1960s—while others have been condemned—such as Richard Nixon's ef-

forts, from 1972 to 1974, to cover up the involvement of his aides in the Watergate scandal.

Most of the truly history-making presidential decisions, though, remain the subject of intense scrutiny and historical debate. Many of these were made during a time of war or other crisis, in which a president was forced to risk either spectacular success or devastating failure. Examples include Lincoln's much-scrutinized handling of the crisis at Fort Sumter, the first conflict of the Civil War; FDR's efforts to aid the European Allies at the beginning of World War II; Harry Truman's controversial decision to use the atomic bomb in order to end that conflict; and Lyndon Johnson's fateful decision to escalate the war in Vietnam.

Each volume in the Presidents and Their Decisions series devotes a full chapter to each of the president's key decisions. The essays in each chapter, most written by presidential historians and biographers, offer a range of perspectives on the president and his actions. Some provide background on the political, social, and economic factors behind a particular decision. Others critique the president's performance, offering a negative or positive appraisal. Essays have been chosen for their concise and engaging presentation of the facts, and each is preceded by a straightforward summary of the article's content.

In addition to the articles, these books include extensive material to help the student researcher. An opening essay provides both a brief biography of the president and an overview of the events that occurred during his time in office. A chronology also helps readers keep track of the dates of specific events. A comprehensive index and an annotated table of contents aid readers in quickly locating material of interest, and an extensive bibliography serves as a launching point for further research. Finally, an appendix of primary historical documents provides a sampling of the president's most important speeches, as well as some of his contemporaries' criticisms.

Greenhaven Press's Presidents and Their Decisions series will help students gain a deeper understanding of the decisions made by some of the most influential leaders in American history.

THEODORE ROOSEVELT:
A BIOGRAPHY

E VEN AMONG PRESIDENTS, THEODORE ROOSEVELT IS A compelling figure. Easily one of the most charismatic and popular presidents ever to serve, Roosevelt embraced what he referred to as "the strenuous life." Distinguishing himself physically and intellectually, he approached the presidency with the same zest he displayed for life, and in so doing thoroughly dominated his times like no other peacetime leader ever would. The robust Roosevelt had a passion for adventure, possessed a formidable intellect, and was a wartime hero who accomplished more during his presidency than perhaps any president to serve before him. One of his contemporaries was moved to comment that the president had "the force and energy of two strong men combined."[1]

Roosevelt was a prolific writer, employing his impressive command of nature, history, politics, and military affairs to pen numerous books over the course of his life. He was a man of both action and letters; few who were as well read as Roosevelt could at the same time claim to have hunted grizzly bears. He was equally comfortable conversing with poets as with cowboys, and boxing came as naturally to him as governance. Indeed, Theodore Roosevelt was a man of great passion, energy, and a seemingly insatiable thirst for intellectual and physical stimulation.

Yet alongside this dashing portrayal of Roosevelt was a complex and controversial president. His ego and ambition were matched in force and conviction only by his sense of honor and dedication to public service. An advocate of peace who was at the same time militaristic, a pragmatic social reformer driven by lofty idealism, and an ardent nationalist with a commitment to progressive programs for the disadvantaged, Roosevelt was a man of seeming contradictions and strong moral convictions. It should be no surprise that, although he enjoyed immense popularity before, during, and after his presidency, he was despised by a sizable segment of the population, including many southern whites, captains of industry, and conservative members of his own Republican Party.

Countless schools have been named after Theodore Roosevelt and both a U.S. federal building and federal courthouse bear his name. A dam and a lake in Arizona, an island in the nation's capital city, and numerous historic sites and memorial parks have been dedicated to Roosevelt. His heroic stature endures and has been honored with everything from the posthumous awarding in 2001 of the Medal of Honor for his valor in battle to Hasbro Corporation's decision to create a Lieutenant Colonel Teddy Roosevelt toy as part of its popular GI Joe collection. It is perhaps fitting that Roosevelt's likeness is carved into Mount Rushmore beside those of George Washington, Thomas Jefferson, and Abraham Lincoln. A century after his presidency, he remains one of the most popular Americans and is routinely rated by presidential historians as one of the ten greatest presidents to serve.[2]

The Early Years

Theodore Roosevelt was born on October 27, 1858, in New York City. He was born into affluence, the second of four children of Theodore and Martha Bulloch Roosevelt. His parents were from prominent families: His father was descended from Dutch stock, and his mother was the daughter of southern gentility. His paternal ancestors, the Van Roosevelts, had emigrated from Holland during the mid-seventeenth century. By all accounts the Roosevelt family was a prosperous and happy one, even though Theodore's mother was a Confederate sympathizer during the Civil War while his father supported the Union.

Poor health in the form of asthma, bouts of illness, and weak eyesight hindered young Roosevelt. As a result, he was educated at home, largely by tutors. However, displaying what would become trademark Rooseveltian traits, young "Teedie" (as he was nicknamed) threw himself with enthusiasm and determination into a vigorous physical, emotional, and intellectual regimen designed to strengthen his body and toughen his resolve. Taking up boxing, weight lifting, and horseback riding, the young boy piled muscle onto his frame and willed himself to excel at all things. He also developed a profound intellectual curiosity and a lifelong love of military history and nature. His fondness of the outdoors and of books was encouraged by his family, which indulged his interests and took him on trips to Europe and the Middle East. It was during his impressionable youth that young Theodore seems to have developed his sense of civic responsibility—"noblesse oblige" to those of his high social class—and strong moral convictions.

In 1876 Roosevelt entered Harvard, where he did well academically, earning membership in the prestigious Phi Beta Kappa society and graduating magna cum laude in 1880. While he was at Harvard, the young student began researching naval history. This project would eventually be published in 1882 as the book *The Naval War of 1812*, which would bring Roosevelt much acclaim and establish him as a literary force. Because of the keen insights revealed in the book, it would become standard reading at military academies and among military historians for years to come.

Marriage and Tragedy

On October 27, 1880, Theodore Roosevelt married Alice Hathaway Lee (born July 29, 1861) from Chestnut Hill, Massachusetts, whom he had met and fallen in love with while at Harvard. Befitting of his character, upon graduating from Harvard he did not wait long to begin a new life. Indeed, many of what would become his lifelong passions and interests as president—literature, politics, nature, military service, the American West, and civic reform—would be bolstered during the period from 1880 to 1884. In addition to publishing the first of many books, it was also then that the young man first entered politics. Roosevelt had been attending Columbia Law School, but he was bored with his classes and chose to pursue a career in politics. Winning a seat as a Republican in the New York State Assembly in 1881 at the tender age of twenty-three, he became the youngest person ever to hold this distinction.

After his term in office in 1882, he served two additional one-year terms. Roosevelt's foray into public life both agreed with him and proved successful, as he won reelection in 1883 by the largest margin of any legislator in the state and became his party's leader. Refusing to bow to the pressures of state party elders, however, the increasingly influential maverick assemblyman was soon stripped of his leadership position by those threatened by his independence, popularity, and unpredictable reforms. But Roosevelt's energetic service had already distinguished him as a reform-minded progressive who supported a number of "good government" initiatives to improve the delivery of public services and the practice of government. He also championed programs designed to improve living and working conditions for the poor. In doing so, he demonstrated the courage to often break with his own party and boldly take on powerful business interests that had gone virtually unchallenged.

It was during this period of his life that he acted upon his fascination with the American West, purchasing two cattle ranches in the Dakota Territory. In 1882 he also launched his military career by joining the National Guard as a second lieutenant and was promoted to the rank of captain the following year.

To Alice and Theodore, a daughter, Alice, was born on February 12, 1884. Sadly, their happy marriage ended abruptly in tragedy when, only two short days after the birth of the Roosevelt's first child, both his wife and his mother died on the same day. Alice succumbed to Bright's disease, a chronic liver disorder, and his mother, Martha, died of typhoid fever. Roosevelt was distraught and dealt with his grief and loneliness by leaving his political career and home in New York to travel west to the Dakota Territory. There, he lived and worked as a rancher, hunted, and wrote history.

A Second Marriage and a Return to Politics

In 1886 Roosevelt returned home, where he ran unsuccessfully for mayor of New York City. That same year he married his childhood friend Edith Kermit (born August 6, 1861) of Norwich, Connecticut, with whom he had corresponded after his first wife's death. The couple was married in London, and the marriage was a solid one, with both partners placing a great deal of stock in intelligence, culture, and their family. Edith was private by nature, but she both accepted and supported her husband's political ambitions, becoming a capable political partner and confidante for him. The Roosevelts had five children: Theodore Jr. (1887–1944), Kermit (1889–1943), Ethel (1891–1977), Archibald (1894–1979), and Quentin (1897–1918).

After devoting himself to writing for several years, Roosevelt accepted an appointment from President Benjamin Harrison as the U.S. Civil Service Commissioner in 1889. His thirst for public service reinvigorated, the reformer set about eliminating the corrupt and inefficient "spoils system" that defined public employment. He promoted competitive examinations for employment, hiring based on merit, ethics in government, and other mechanisms to improve the public workforce, once again refusing to allow opposition from powerful interests to derail his work. When the Democratic challenger, Grover Cleveland, defeated President Harrison, the new president chose to retain Roosevelt as his commissioner. This action served as testimony to the success of Roosevelt's reforms and the respect Cleveland had for the former New York assemblyman with whom he had worked many years before while serving as the state's governor. In 1895 Roosevelt returned to New York to become the city's police commissioner. Facing widespread corruption and an undisciplined police force, Roosevelt took on city leaders, businesses, organized crime, and often his own officers in instituting ethical reforms, training, and improved operations.

The Spanish-American War

Roosevelt's long-standing passion for military adventure was fulfilled in 1897 when he was appointed assistant secretary of the navy by President William McKinley. Roosevelt was descended from a long and proud family line of able seamen and naval officers, and he hungered for the opportunity to serve militarily. His tenure was noteworthy for advocating a stronger, better prepared naval force and a desire to see the Caribbean and Latin America liberated from the yoke of Spanish colonialism.

His views were shaped by a belief that today seems outdated and even racist. Roosevelt felt that it was the right, if not the duty, of "superior" nations to assist or dictate to—depending on the need—"inferior" ones.[3] Although such actions might involve war or the imposition of outside political control, Roosevelt believed the end goal of bringing civilization to "lesser" peoples would not only help those in question, but humanity would also be served. Further motivation came from what he saw as a sense of moral purpose in his beliefs and actions and the inherent rightness of the United States and all that it stood for. To achieve his objectives, Roosevelt even maneuvered behind the scenes to bring about conflict with Spain in order to justify eliminating its colonial presence in places like Cuba.

After the sinking of the *Maine* while the ship was in Havana's harbor in 1898, hostilities broke out between the

United States and Spain. Roosevelt promptly resigned his post in McKinley's administration in May 1898 to join the fight. Although he longed to spar and test his mettle under fire, regular military service in the Spanish-American War would not do for Roosevelt. He needed something on a grander, more romantic scale. Accordingly, he organized his own unit: the First U.S. Volunteer Cavalry Regiment, which would become known as the Rough Riders. Under Lieutenant Colonel Roosevelt, an eclectic unit of cowboys, Indians, former college students and athletes, and New York police officers was brought together under a commander determined to defeat the enemy and achieve glory.

To assure his aspirations, joining the unit were Roosevelt's own publicists, who were charged with documenting the Rough Riders' heroic exploits. On July 1, 1898, U.S. forces—including Roosevelt's Rough Riders—had encircled and attacked fortified hills near Santiago, Cuba. During the battle that ensued, Roosevelt led the Rough Riders in a heroic and daring charge up Kettle Hill, an act that nearly killed him but won him the wartime reputation he long desired. The Rough Riders made it up the hill and flanked the Spanish troops on San Juan Hill. One year after his service, Roosevelt published an account of the Rough Riders.

Governor and Vice President

Roosevelt's military exploits were told throughout the country and translated into political office for the Rough Rider. Returning triumphant to New York, he was elected governor in 1898. Once again, the reformer emerged, challenging his own party, big business, and the forces of corruption while fighting for groundbreaking reforms. Corporations were taxed, antidiscrimination laws were enacted, natural resources were protected, and labor disputes were mediated. All the while his popularity and the Roosevelt mystique grew. Although he encountered bitter opposition from big business and New York's "political machine," he had gained national attention and emerged as perhaps the country's foremost political reformer.

President McKinley's vice president, Garret Hobart, had died in 1899, and the number-two spot on McKinley's reelection ticket in 1900 remained open. For all of his fame, Roosevelt was an unlikely choice to be vice president: The president seemed cautiously uncertain about Roosevelt; the political establishment and corporations were wary of his progressivism and considered him a reckless cowboy; and the prospective candidate himself was hesitant to leave the governorship—a job he loved—for the obscure and powerless office of vice president. Moreover, he was barely into his forties. But the office would provide Roosevelt with a stepping-stone to the presidency (he had his sights on the 1904 election), and anti-Roosevelt forces in New York saw the move as a way to rid themselves of his reforms.

In November 1900 the McKinley-Roosevelt ticket won in a landslide election, and in March 1901 Theodore Roosevelt assumed the office of vice president. Only a few months later, on September 6, 1901, President McKinley was shot in Buffalo, New York, while attending the Pan American Exposition. At the time, Roosevelt was vacationing in the Adirondack Mountains in New York and, on news of the assassination attempt, rushed to join the president, only to arrive after McKinley's passing. Roosevelt was sworn in as the nation's twenty-sixth president on September 14, 1901, taking the oath of office in Buffalo. At the age of forty-two, he became the youngest president in the history of the country.

The First Presidential Term (1901–1905)

Because he was not elected to the nation's highest office but became president as a result of McKinley's assassination, Roosevelt felt a certain obligation to continue the policies of his predecessor and even retain the same cabinet. Nonetheless, it was not long before the young chief executive began to put his own stamp on the presidency. Just as McKinley had an internationalist foreign policy, Roosevelt also sought a very active and engaged role for the United States. However, unlike his predecessor, Roosevelt undertook a variety of initiatives that both contributed to and affirmed the rise of the United States as a world power. In addition, although the Republican Party was generally considered to be pro-business and to favor large corporations, Roosevelt endeavored to implement a more balanced approach toward the economy. Finally, throughout both of his terms, he worked to raise public awareness about the environment and aggressively sought to conserve and preserve the nation's natural wonders.

Roosevelt's Foreign Policy

As a result of the Spanish-American War, the United States had expanded its interests in the Caribbean and Latin America. For instance, the United States had gained the territory of Puerto Rico and had stationed troops in Cuba to help that country make the transition from Spanish colony to independent nation. Early in his tenure, the young president demonstrated the growing influence of the United States in the region. Roosevelt showed his support for the Monroe Doctrine, which held that European influence should be kept out of the Western Hemisphere, when he intervened to settle a dispute between Venezuela and three European powers. Germany, Italy, and Great Britain had established a blockade of the country in order to force the Venezuelan government to pay its debts, whereupon Roosevelt dispatched a naval flotilla to the area and ultimately forced the Europeans to withdraw.

One other manifestation of Roosevelt's more assertive foreign policy was a renewed American interest in building a canal across the isthmus of Panama. Such a canal would have significant potential economic and strategic benefits.

It would dramatically reduce the amount of time necessary for ships to travel from the East Coast to the West Coast of the United States and vice versa, and thus allow the country to assert itself in both the Atlantic and the Pacific. Since the French effort to construct a canal had failed, Roosevelt faced detractors who doubted the project would succeed. Undeterred, he also wanted to ensure that any canal would be built and controlled by the United States.

At that time, Panama was a province of Colombia. When the Colombian Senate rejected a treaty to build the canal, Roosevelt helped foster a revolution in Panama by dispatching American troops to support the rebellion. The president justified his actions by asserting that Colombia was ruled by a dictator, and Panamanians were therefore controlled by a government "without their consent."[4] He

---

The Bear Facts

The teddy bear, that perennial playtime favorite of small children, was named after Theodore Roosevelt. A legend developed having to do with the events of a hunting trip, a bear, and the president. Wilson Quarterly *examines the legend and reveals the truth behind it.*

The myth was irresistible: On a hunt in the Mississippi Delta in 1902, the exuberant sportsman-president Theodore Roosevelt came upon a black bear that had been captured by a member of his party. Roosevelt refused to take the life of the helpless animal. The nation heard the story. To commemorate the event, a woman named Rose Michtom in Brooklyn made, and immediately sold, a couple of bears stuffed with excelsior and fitted with shoe-button eyes. Her husband, Morris, wrote the president asking for permission to market a line of the toy animals as "Teddy Bears." The president apparently said yes, and in no time at all the Michtoms couldn't

contended that U.S. military support was designed to promote democracy. When Panama became independent, Roosevelt's first secretary of state, John Hay, was able to negotiate the Hay-Bunau-Varilla Treaty, which gave the United States the right to construct a canal across the isthmus. In addition, the United States was granted sovereignty over a ten-mile-wide corridor through which the canal would ultimately flow. In return, the United States paid Panama $10 million and pledged an annual payment of $250,000. The canal was completed in 1914. During its construction, in November 1906, Roosevelt traveled to oversee the work and became the first president to travel outside of the United States while serving in office.

Roosevelt continued to use the rhetoric of fostering democracy as a rationale for military and economic inter-

---

keep up with the orders. They earned a fortune. The country took the teddy bear to heart, and kids took it to bed, where it has been a cuddly comfort ever since.

What actually happened during that 1902 hunt, according to Douglas Brinkley writing in *Oxford American* (November/December 2000), might not have sent Rose Michtom so quickly to the excelsior bin. There was a captured bear. But by the time Roosevelt happened upon the beast, it had crushed one of the hunting dogs to death and seriously wounded two others, and its own skull had been smashed by the butt of a rifle. The bear was unconscious and tied to a tree. Roosevelt refused under circumstances so dismaying to a true huntsman to shoot the bear. Instead, he had it put out of its misery by another member of the party, who used a bowie knife to slit the bear's throat. The carcass was draped across a horse and removed.

It was on its way into history—and the nursery.

"Findings," *Wilson Quarterly,* vol. 25, issue 1, Winter 2001, pp. 4–5.

vention. He developed what became known as the Roosevelt Corollary to the Monroe Doctrine, which asserted the right of the United States to intervene in countries in the Caribbean and Latin America to prevent similar interference by European powers. Accordingly, he dispatched troops to Santo Domingo in 1904 to protect it from European intervention. Roosevelt believed that the United States had a duty to act in order to promote democracy in these areas while European powers such as France and Germany were mainly interested in exploiting these countries for economic or strategic interests.

The Square Deal

Just as Roosevelt embarked upon a more aggressive foreign policy, his domestic policies reflected the progressive activism that had been a hallmark of his political career. Like many other progressives, he rejected the Jeffersonian notion of limited government and instead embraced a Hamiltonian vision of a strong central government in order to regulate the growing and increasingly complex American economy. Under Roosevelt, the federal government became more involved in the regulation of the economy—a trend that continued throughout the twentieth century. Roosevelt's actions also ensured that, for the first time since the tenure of Abraham Lincoln, the executive branch, and not the legislature, would be the dominant branch of government.

Roosevelt's economic policies had their greatest impact in two areas: labor relations and the regulation of trusts and monopolies. Soon after becoming president, he became involved in efforts to settle a bitter strike by coal miners in Pennsylvania. Although his initial offer to arbitrate the strike was rejected by the mine owners, Roosevelt utilized his considerable influence on public opinion to pressure both sides to accept a settlement. The deal raised the pay of the miners and reduced their workday to nine hours, but it also offered concessions to the mine owners. As a result, Roosevelt was able to claim that both sides received a "square deal," a phrase that became a slogan for the young president. The episode also reinforced Roosevelt's popularity and his credentials as a reformer.

While he worked to settle the coal strike, Roosevelt also embarked on a broad campaign to break up trusts and monopolies whose unrivaled leverage harmed the economy. Roosevelt did distinguish between what he perceived to be "good" trusts, those that stimulated the economy by lowering prices, and "bad" trusts, or those that manipulated prices and wages for their benefit.[5] On February 19, 1902, the President ordered an antitrust suit to dissolve the Northern Securities Company under the auspices of the Sherman Antitrust Act. Ultimately, the Roosevelt administration would undertake forty-five antitrust actions and firmly establish the role of the federal government in regulating the economy. A further sign of Roosevelt's commitment to government regulation of the economy was the establishment of the Department of Commerce and Labor in February 1903.

Conservation

Roosevelt achieved perhaps his most lasting success in environmental policy. Soon after becoming president, he demonstrated his commitment to conservation by designating Crater Lake in Oregon as a national park on May 22, 1902. However, the environmentally conscious Roosevelt found that conservative members of his own party often opposed his conservation efforts. Consequently, he waged a two-tiered environmental campaign, whereby he used the executive powers of his office to put territory aside for conservation while also taking his message directly to the American people in an effort to rally public support for his cause and thus put pressure on members of Congress concerned about pleasing their constituents.

Roosevelt followed the establishment of Crater Lake National Park with the Newlands Reclamation Act on June 17, 1903, which was the first of twenty-one federal irrigation projects. Later that year, the president designated Pelican Island in Florida as the first of fifty-one federal bird sanctuaries he established.

The Second Presidential Term (1905–1909)

Roosevelt campaigned diligently to be reelected in 1904. He saw the election both as a test of public approval for his policies and as a mandate on whether to expand his reformist platform. He won the election against Democratic challenger Alton B. Parker by a landslide of both the popular vote and electoral college votes.[6] Roosevelt felt that the election vindicated his policy choices, and his second term was marked by further progressive initiatives.

Armed with the electoral mandate, he expanded his conservation campaign and consistently brought new areas under federal protection. The U.S. Forest Service was created in 1905, and in 1908 Roosevelt designated the Grand Canyon as a national monument and federal game preserve. He also convened the first conference of the nation's governors in 1908 to study the problems of conservation and environmental protection. Despite some continuing congressional opposition from both parties, by the time Roosevelt had left office, he had tripled the size of national forests from 50 million acres to 150 million acres. He had also created five national parks, numerous national monuments, and more than fifty wildlife refuges.

Roosevelt continued and even expanded his progressive economic policies. In 1906 Roosevelt signed the Hepburn Act, which gave the Interstate Commerce Commission expanded powers to regulate the railroads. That same year, he signed the Pure Food and Drug Act, giving the federal government the power to inspect meat and other consumer products.

Although he had a number of notable successes, Roosevelt faced increasing political opposition from conservative Republican congressmen. Led by Speaker of the House Joseph Cannon and Senators Nelson Aldrich and Orville Platt, a group of conservative or "stalwart" Republicans in both houses of Congress worked together to defeat some of Roosevelt's more liberal economic and environmental policies. In response, the president attempted to bypass Congress by again appealing directly to the people. Roosevelt even established an office for the press within the White House to interact with the press more efficiently. His skillful management of the press served as a model for later presidents, including Franklin Roosevelt, the famous husband of his favorite niece, Eleanor.

Foreign Policy

Although he continued his domestic reforms, many of Roosevelt's most significant achievements during his second term were in foreign policy. He endeavored to conduct the nation's diplomacy in a manner that confirmed the great power status of the United States. For instance, in 1905 he offered to mediate an end to the Russo-Japanese War. The result was the Treaty of Portsmouth, which ended the conflict and earned Roosevelt the Nobel Peace Prize for his role. (He was the first American to win a Nobel Prize in any category.) Roosevelt utilized the fame and credibility gained by his actions to also mediate a Franco-German dispute over influence in Morocco in 1906.

Long before he became president, Roosevelt perceived that the nation needed to increase the size and capability of its navy. He read and was greatly influenced by Alfred Thayer Mahan's *The Influence of Sea Power Upon History, 1669–1783*, and he became a staunch advocate of the need for the United States to become a global naval power. The acquisition of and need to protect new territories in the Caribbean and Pacific following the Spanish-American

War reinforced Roosevelt's belief that the nation needed a powerful navy. As president, Roosevelt also foresaw the rise of German and Japanese naval power and its detrimental consequences to American interests. He recognized that the United States would need naval forces to protect its interests in both the Atlantic and the Pacific. Roosevelt's impact on the U.S. Navy was in many ways greater than that of any other president. For instance, a champion of innovation, he became a proponent of submarine use as an adjunct to the navy's military preparedness.

Even though Roosevelt perceived that Germany was the most significant threat to American interests, tensions between the United States and Japan increased during his second term. Anti-immigrant sentiment in California, Oregon, and Washington resulted in a backlash against Japanese Americans. In 1906 the "Gentlemen's Agreement" reduced immigration and repealed some anti-immigrant legislation in the states, easing the strained relations between the two nations. Nonetheless, Roosevelt became determined to undertake actions that would demonstrate the military power of the United States in the Pacific.

The Great White Fleet

Roosevelt's concern with Japan led him to embark on an ambitious plan: He would dispatch an American fleet to circumnavigate the globe. This would demonstrate to the world the ability of the United States to project its naval power anywhere in the world. The naval force, which was known as the Great White Fleet because the ships were painted white, consisted of sixteen battleships with dozens of escort vessels and some eighteen thousand sailors and marines. Initially, Roosevelt faced some domestic opposition from Congress and even the Navy Department because of concerns that the voyage might provoke the Japanese. Nonetheless, he proceeded with his plans.

The fleet departed from the naval station in Norfolk,

Virginia, on December 16, 1907. The voyage itself was not completed until February 22, 1909. The trip was a resounding success. The naval voyage confirmed the military power of the United States to nations around the world, including Japan, and it was very popular with the American public.

A Continuation of the Strenuous Life

Although he could have run for another term, Roosevelt decided to follow the tradition established by Washington and leave office after his second term. He handpicked his successor, William Howard Taft, who was also known as a progressive reformer. With the popular Roosevelt behind him, Taft easily won election against the Democratic candidate, William Jennings Bryan.

After campaigning for Taft, Roosevelt thought it would be best for his successor if he disappeared from the political scene. Accordingly, in March 1909 Roosevelt and his son Kermit departed for a safari in Africa. The safari was followed by a tour of Europe, where Roosevelt officially received his Nobel Prize. Where he returned to the United States, Roosevelt initially attempted to remain out of the public eye, but he grew increasingly dissatisfied with Taft, who had become too conservative for the former president's tastes. As a result, Roosevelt decided to again run for the Republican presidential nomination in the 1912 election, opposing Taft.

Although Roosevelt won all but one primary and caucus, his delegates were refused admittance to the Republican National Convention in Chicago. Instead, conservatives within the party renominated Taft. Roosevelt then accepted the nomination of the Progressive Party (which came to be known as the Bull Moose Party). Roosevelt campaigned vigorously and even managed to deliver a speech in Milwaukee after being shot during an assassination attempt. However, Roosevelt and Taft split the Republican vote, and the Democratic candidate, Woodrow Wilson, won the election.[7]

Following the loss, Roosevelt continued writing, published his autobiography, and went on a lengthy expedition in Brazil in 1914 that nearly killed him. After his return, Roosevelt publicly supported America's entry into World War I on the side of the Allies. Once the United States entered the war in 1917, Roosevelt even volunteered to raise and lead an army division, but he was turned down by President Wilson. All of Roosevelt's sons served during the war. On July 16, 1918, the Roosevelt family received the news that Quentin had been shot down and killed while serving as a pilot in France. Roosevelt's health had been in decline since his return from the Brazilian excursion, and Quentin's death seemed to hasten his demise. By the fall of 1918, Roosevelt was increasingly confined to bed. On January 6, 1919, Roosevelt died in his sleep at his home, Sagamore Hill, of an arterial blood clot.

Legacy

Textbooks on politics and government generally point to Franklin D. Roosevelt's presidency (1933–1945) as the start of what has been called the modern era of the office. However, a compelling argument can be made that it was Theodore Roosevelt who ushered in the modern presidency. The country's twenty-sixth president, for example, was the first to "go public," using his immense popularity to appeal directly to the American people for support of his programs, something that all presidents in recent times have done. Roosevelt understood and harnessed the power of the media. He crafted his message and public image in a manner unlike any president who served before him and with a sense of media savvy befitting modern-day presidents. He was also the first to truly embrace the notion that the United States should play a prominent role in international affairs, and his policies reflected this belief. In actions heretofore unheard-of for an American president, Roosevelt sent the U.S. Navy to circumnavigate the globe, called for the country to build the Panama Canal, mediated peace between warring nations, and pursued an array of other diplomatic endeavors. It is perhaps fitting that Theodore Roosevelt began his historic presidency in the year 1901, at the dawn of what would come to be called the American century.

Roosevelt's policies and decisions as president reflected his personal philosophy and his pursuit of the strenuous life. In domestic politics, he worked for an expanded role for the federal government in regulating business and in promoting conservation. His economic policy sought to balance the interests of business and industry with the needs of consumers and workers. As such, Roosevelt became the first president to securely establish a legitimate role for government in regulating the economy. Concurrently, he elevated the importance of conservation and environmental policy to a level unseen prior to his tenure. Not only did Roosevelt dramatically expand the amount of territory under federal protection, but he also helped ensure that the public recognized the importance of the environment.

In foreign policy, Roosevelt consistently endeavored to elevate the status of the United States in the world. His decision to undertake construction of the Panama Canal was met by opposition in the United States, especially because of American participation in the Panamanian revolution. Nonetheless, he used the construction project as a means to confirm the capabilities of the United States and to affirm the domination of the nation in the Western Hemisphere. The president then used the voyage of the Great White Fleet to demonstrate the military power of the United States to the rest of the world. Roosevelt's actions initiated the dramatic expansion of power, both domestically and internationally, that would set the stage for the American century.

Notes

1. Quoted in Lyman Gage, *Memoirs of Lyman Gage.* New York: House of Field, 1937, p. 142.

2. For examples of presidential rankings, see Douglas A. Lonnstrom and Thomas O. Kelly II, "Rating the Presidents: A Tracking Study," *Presidential Studies Quarterly,* Fall 1997, pp. 591–98; Robert K. Murray, "The Murray Poll," *Journal of American History,* December 1982; Arthur Schlesinger Sr., "The U.S. Presidents," *Life,* 1948; Arthur Schlesinger Sr., "Our Presidents: A Rating by 75 Scholars," *New York Times Magazine,* July 29, 1962; Siena Research Institute Poll, Siena College, New York, 1994.

3. David H. Burton, *Theodore Roosevelt: Confident Imperialist.* Philadelphia: University of Pennsylvania Press, 1968.

4. Theodore Roosevelt, *Theodore Roosevelt: An Autobiography.* 1913. Reprint, New York: Da Capo, 1985, p. 533.

5. H.W. Brands, *T.R.: The Last Romantic.* New York: BasicBooks, 1997, p. 438.

6. Roosevelt received 7.6 million votes to Parker's 5.1 million, and 336 electoral votes to Parker's 140.

7. Wilson received 6.3 million popular votes and 435 electoral votes, while Roosevelt came in second with 4.1 million popular votes and 88 electoral votes, and Taft came in third with 3.5 million popular votes and 8 electoral votes.

CHAPTER

1

ROOSEVELT AND THE BIRTH OF CONSERVATION

Roosevelt Helped Establish American Environmentalism

Sandy Marvinney

This essay presents Theodore Roosevelt as a visionary who was able to arouse and rally the nation's awareness regarding the need to stop the destruction of natural resources. At the time Roosevelt became president, virtually no federal measures existed to prevent the wholesale destruction of forests, the land, and ecosystems. His presidency marks the first viable attempt to protect natural resources. Roosevelt placed thousands of acres of public land under federal protection, established more than fifty wildlife refuges, expanded the national park system, and set aside millions of acres of timberlands. Author Sandy Marvinney has written on conservation and environmental issues.

TEDDY ROOSEVELT—SPEAK SOFTLY AND CARRY A BIG STICK, trust busting, rough riding, big game hunting President. More dimly do our high school history book memories recall Roosevelt the conservationist and guardian of the nation's resources. Even more dimly, if at all, do we remember Roosevelt the naturalist, the highly respected authority on animal and bird life who often interrupted White House meetings to rush to the window to identify a bird singing on the lawn.

Excerpted from "Theodore Roosevelt, Conservationist," by Sandy Marvinney, *New York State Conservationist*, June 1972. Copyright © 1972 by *New York State Conservationist*. Reprinted with permission.

Yet it is the naturalist Roosevelt which defines the man as well as any other facet of his versatile character, and from the perspective of the environmental consciousness of the '70s his efforts in the field of conservation are perhaps the greatest legacy of his presidency.

Roosevelt was one of a handful of farsighted men who strove to awaken the country to the consequences of unchecked destruction of the nation's forests, land and resources at a time when the average American thought little about such problems and cared less. Roosevelt was a conservationist not because it would win him any votes, but because it was rooted in his nature and his active perception of the world about him.

An Education in Conservation

The Roosevelt who cherished the hidden spirit of the wilderness came to his love of nature in early youth, exploring the woods and fields on excursions to the country from his New York City home, on family vacations in the Adirondacks, and later on along the shores of Long Island when the family moved to Oyster Bay.

At the age of nine Theodore founded the "Roosevelt Natural History Museum," a collection of bird nests, animal skulls, insects, shells and minerals collected on his outdoor adventures. He read precociously all the natural history works he could get his hands on and kept voluminous diaries on his field experiences, recording detailed observations on bird and animal life.

Roosevelt was a self-taught naturalist, epitomizing the sentiments of his friend of later life, naturalist/author John Burroughs who wrote that "To absorb a thing is better than to learn it, and we absorb what we enjoy . . . the way of knowledge of nature is the way of love and enjoyment, and is more surely found in the open air than in the schoolroom or laboratory."

He entered Harvard in the fall of 1876 intent on becoming a natural scientist in the tradition of [John James] Audubon. Upon finding that the way of scientific knowledge at Harvard was through the microscope and laboratory, Roosevelt's ambitions cooled. He found no academic outlet for his enthusiasm for field study and when his interests were eventually drawn to political economy he decided to make politics his career.

Nevertheless, Roosevelt still found time for scientific pursuits and in 1877 he and a Harvard friend published a small leaflet entitled "The Summer Birds of the Adirondack Mountains in Franklin County, N. Y."—his first contribution to zoological literature.

During his college years Roosevelt frequently vacationed in Maine where two experienced northwoods guides took the young naturalist under their wing and greatly expanded his experience and knowledge of hunting, trapping, camping and survival in the wilds. Roosevelt soon outgrew his scrawny, illness-plagued youth and acquired the strength and indomitable energy that characterized all his ventures.

The Naturalist Politician

In 1881 Roosevelt won election to the New York State Assembly, embarking upon his political career. The following year he made his first trip west to the Dakotas where he bought a ranch. Captivated by the open spaces and fast disappearing traces of wildness, Roosevelt spent the next ten years dividing his time between East and West, exploring the Dakotas and the Rocky Mountain states.

During this period he authored two books, "Hunting Trips of a Ranchman" and "The Wilderness Hunter," which received favorable reviews. According to C. Hart Merriam, Chief of the U.S. Biological Survey, Roosevelt was an authority on the life histories of big game animals and was regarded as one of the outstanding field naturalists of his day. He has been described as "the first and last President of the United States to have a biological sense of proportions—to know the importance of everything from forests to birds, from hybridization to plant introduction."

At the time Roosevelt moved into prominence in national politics, conservation was a practically unknown word and the federal government had taken only a few halting steps in its direction. The myth that America was a land of inexhaustible natural wealth died hard and until the latter part of the nineteenth century there was little concern that the country would run out of its vast timber supply, fertile soils and seemingly unbounded mineral resources. Land was there for all who wanted it and the government seemed devoted to helping private citizens exploit these resources without restriction.

Resource preservation was almost exclusively the concern of a few scientists and recently established specialized organizations such as the American Forestry Association and the Audubon Society. One such group, the Boone and Crockett Club, was founded in 1888 by Roosevelt and several other dedicated sportsmen who were concerned about preserving big game species and their habitat. Roosevelt served as president of the club from 1888 to 1894 and under his leadership it became one of the most effective conservation organizations of its day.

The first federal initiative in resource preservation occurred in 1872 with the establishment of Yellowstone National Park, just ahead of a threatened invasion of homesteaders. Rapid depletion of America's forests provided the impetus for broader federal programs. By the end of the nineteenth century an estimated half of the original forest cover of nearly one billion acres had been lost and in 1891 Congress finally enacted a far-reaching law authorizing the President to withdraw land from the public domain to create forest reserves under the jurisdiction of the Interior Department.

The movement for forest preservation in New York was

well established but nonetheless foundering in bureaucratic inefficiency when Roosevelt became Governor in 1898. Although he served for only two years before becoming

Roosevelt Visits Yosemite

Prize-winning Roosevelt scholar Edmund Morris describes his subject's love for the outdoors as being "bully!" which was quite apparent on Roosevelt's famous trip to Yosemite.

Roosevelt lay high in Yosemite, on a bed of fragrant pine needles, looking up at the sky. On all sides soared the cinnamon-colored shafts of sequoia trees. He had the feeling that he was "lying in a great solemn cathedral, far vaster and more beautiful than any built by the hands of man." Birdsong filled the arches as the sky darkened. He identified the treble *tessitura* of hermit thrushes, and thought it "an appropriate choir for such a place of worship."

His companion was John Muir, the glaciologist, naturalist, and founder of the Sierra Club. Since early youth, Muir had roamed Yosemite, carrying little more than "some bread and tea in an old sock," returning to civilization as infrequently as possible. At sixty-five, he knew more about the park, and loved it more passionately, than any other American. Roosevelt had booked his exclusive services well in advance: "I want to drop politics absolutely for four days, and just be out in the open with you."

The President was disappointed to find that Muir had no ear for bird music. He was Wordsworthian rather than Keatsian, revering only "rocks and stones and trees." Garrulous, erudite, and wall-eyed, he talked a pure form of preservation that Roosevelt was not used to hearing. He had no patience with the utilitarian "greatest good for the greatest number" policy of Chief Forester Gifford Pinchot, the President's very good friend. *Con*servation favored business at the expense of nature, and property rather than beauty. "The

Vice President in 1900, Roosevelt devoted considerable attention to conservation problems. "All that I strove for in the nation in connection with conservation was fore-

'greatest number' is too often found to be number one."

Whatever resonance such views found in the President's own developing awareness of the "democracy" of national parks, he would have preferred to hear less of Muir and more of the hermit thrushes. Eventually he fell asleep, in the piney air. Another bird chorale saluted him at dawn.

For the next forty-eight hours, the boy in Roosevelt, never quite suppressed, reveled in his wild surroundings. "This is bully!" he yelled, when Muir burned a dead tree for him and the sparks hurtled skyward. After another night out, he awoke at Glacier Point, and was intrigued to find himself buried under four inches of snow. "This is bullier!"

On 17 May he came down from the peaks in dusty khakis, his eyes sparkling. "I never felt better in my life!" Muir, too, was elated, having confessedly fallen in love with the President's "interesting, hearty and manly" personality. The substance of their camping conversations remained tacit, suggesting some philosophical difference on the subject of Gifford Pinchot. Muir won at least an immediate presidential order to extend the California forest through the Mount Shasta region, and a promise that Yosemite's over-commercialized valley would be ceded back to the national park system. Roosevelt's next conservation statement, on 19 May, was obstinately utilitarian, yet an eloquent plea later that day echoed the preservationist sentiments he had expressed at the Grand Canyon. Speaking in Sacramento, he begged Californians to preserve their "marvelous natural resources" unimpaired. "We are not building this country of ours for a day. It is to last through the ages."

Edmund Morris, *Theodore Rex*. New York: Random House, 2001, pp. 229–31.

shadowed by what I strove to obtain for New York State when I was Governor," he wrote in his autobiography.

Land in the Catskills and Adirondacks had been set aside as forest preserve in 1886 under jurisdiction of a forest commission which proved weak in the administration of its duties. Timber interests maintained a free hand and widespread lumber stealing was carried on in utter contempt for the law. The 1883 prohibition against sale of State forest lands was freely circumvented and within 10 years 100,000 acres had been lost from the preserves.

By 1894 public confidence in the forest commission reached an all-time low, arousing strong sentiments for constitutional provisions to safeguard the forests. In that year the Legislature enacted Section 7 Article II of the Constitution—the "forever wild" clause forbidding the sale or lease of any forest preserve land and the sale, removal or destruction of timber.

Forging an Environmental Record

The five-man Fisheries, Game and Forest Commission, a haven for political favoritism, presented the greatest obstacle to efficient management of the preserves. Roosevelt made it clear he wanted to replace the board with a single commissioner to improve administration and inhibit political influences. Although he was unable to impress the merits of this plan on the Republican machine, he did succeed in replacing the five commissioners with competent men of his own choosing who gave the activities of the commission closer scrutiny. In 1900 it was renamed the Forest, Fish and Game Commission in a reordering of priorities and plans were drawn up to improve the management of the preserves.

During his term as Governor Roosevelt sought the advice of Gifford Pinchot, head of the Bureau of Forestry in the Department of Agriculture who later became one of Roosevelt's most trusted presidential advisors. Pinchot was not exceedingly popular among New York conservationists as he favored "conservative lumbering" in the forest preserves and considered the forever wild clause an unprogressive step away from scientific management of the forests.

Pinchot's arguments impressed Roosevelt and he drew upon them for his annual message to the Legislature in 1900. He called attention to the urgent need for scientific study and management of the preserves although emphasizing that until lumbering was carried out along these principles "we cannot afford to suffer it at all in the State forests. Unrestrained greed means the ruin of the great woods and the drying up of the sources of the rivers."

In this same message Roosevelt stressed the importance of controlling forest fires, increasing the number of trained and qualified game wardens and the need for sound administration of the game laws. True to his ornithological interests he called for the protection of ordinary birds, especially songbirds, urging the adoption of a law to prohibit use of skins and feathers in the manufacture of wearing apparel.

During his governorship Roosevelt also expressed concern over the growing pollution of the State's waterways, many of which had become "little more than open sewers." In 1899 he issued an order prohibiting the discharge of untreated sewage, domestic waste, or manufacturing refuse into Saratoga Lake or its tributaries, citing it as a nuisance which interfered with the fullest enjoyment of property rights of landowners along the lake.

The waters of Saratoga emptied into Fish Creek, which flowed into the Hudson River, the source of drinking water for many communities. Roosevelt foresightedly commented that the pollution of the Hudson presented "one of the most perplexing and serious problems affecting the life and health of the people of the State." He ordered the villages of Saratoga Springs and Ballston Spa to install sewage treatment works and ordered the tanneries and pulp mills in the area to render their wastes innocuous before discharging them into the waters.

Sewage treatment was in its infancy in New York in the 1890s and it is unlikely that the Governor's order, probably one of the first of its kind in the State, aroused the offending parties to action. Nevertheless, it did point the finger at a problem that was to receive increasing attention in later years.

First Conservationist President

Roosevelt was vacationing in the Adirondacks near Mt. Marcy when McKinley died of an assassin's bullet on September 14, 1901. Plunging into the responsibilities of the Presidency, Roosevelt saw as one of his most important tasks the development of coherent policies to safeguard the nation's resources.

Roosevelt found in government service a number of far-sighted men such as Pinchot, John Wesley Powell of the U.S. Geological Survey, and Frederick H. Newell of the Reclamation Service who had also identified a need for vigorous federal programs. In Roosevelt they discovered a President who enthusiastically supported their ideas and lent the full power of his office to the implementation of strong conservation measures.

First turning his attention to the reclamation of arid western lands, Roosevelt firmly backed Senator Francis Newland's bill for the development of federal projects to irrigate public lands. The bill was signed into law in June 1902 and by the end of Roosevelt's Presidency in 1909 reclamation was an unqualified success with 30 federal projects completed and over 3,000,000 acres of land under irrigation.

In his first message to Congress Roosevelt stressed the urgency of bringing some rational order to the administration of the forest reserves. The Bureau of Forestry in the Agriculture Department employed all the trained foresters in the government service but had no jurisdiction over the forests, while a division of the General Land-Office in the Interior Department administered the reserves without foresters.

In early 1905 Roosevelt succeeded in transferring jurisdiction over forest lands from the Interior Department to the newly organized U.S. Forest Service headed by Pinchot. During his administration Roosevelt added 150,000,000 acres of timberland to the reserves, tripling the amount set aside by his predecessors. This did not occur without bitter opposition from western lumber and development interests, but an extensive public education program conducted by the Forest Service fostered widespread support for the forest reserve concept as a means of increasing and sustaining the nation's timber resources for the welfare of all the people.

Roosevelt also set aside for federal protection thousands of acres of public land valuable for its mineral wealth or potential for water power development. He exercised particular foresight in creating the first federal wildlife refuge at Pelican Island, Florida to protect egrets threatened with extinction by hunters. By 1909 Roosevelt had established an additional 50 refuges, forming the basis for a federal wildlife protection program that today includes several hundred sanctuaries encompassing millions of acres of land across the country.

In addition Roosevelt added five new parks to the national park system and under the National Monuments Act of 1906 set aside [16 million] acres of unique natural or historic value including California's Muir Woods, Wyoming's Devils Tower, Arizona's Petrified Forest and the Grand Canyon.

Conservation Legacy

Towards the end of his second term Roosevelt focused his attention on the development of a comprehensive conservation program on a national scale. The Inland Waterways Commission which Roosevelt had established in 1907 suggested calling a conference on all aspects of conservation and he enthusiastically seized upon the idea.

The conference, held in Washington in May 1908, was attended by the Governors of all the states, members of Congress, the Cabinet, the Supreme Court and nationally prominent conservationists and scientists. The first meeting of its kind, it gave considerable momentum and prestige to the conservation effort, turning it into a full fledged movement.

Delivering the opening address, Roosevelt called the reckless depletion of natural resources "the weightiest problem before the nation," and urged the participants to join together in a common effort to coordinate a conservation plan.

As an outgrowth of the conference, conservation commissions were created in 36 states and a National Conservation Commission was set up to inventory the nation's water, mineral, land and forest resources. The conference stimulated such great interest that Roosevelt convened a North American Conference in February 1909 attended by delegates from the U.S., Canada and Mexico. From this meeting came the far-reaching statement that natural resources are not confined by national boundaries and no nation acting alone can adequately conserve them.

In retrospect, Theodore Roosevelt is a classic example of a man of unique talents and perception coinciding with the demands of a particular time and place in history. With his understanding of man's dependence on the natural environment and his potential for destroying or protecting that environment, Roosevelt quickly grasped the problems at hand, sought far-reaching answers and gave the nation a firm shove in the direction of wiser management of its natural heritage.

Although Roosevelt did not originate the concept of

conservation he became one of its strongest advocates, and with the authority of the Presidency behind him he perhaps contributed more to the "spreading of the faith" than any other individual of his generation. Today's resurgence of environmental awareness traces a few roots to the foundation of concern laid by early eco-activists in the tradition of Teddy Roosevelt.

Roosevelt Introduced Conservation into American Politics

Harold Howland

In his first annual message to Congress, Roosevelt stressed the importance of the nation's natural resources. He also made clear his intention to take steps to protect the environment. Harold Howland argues that it was in fact Roosevelt who put the terms "reclamation" and "conservation" into American politics. Howland also contends that one of the most important aspects of Roosevelt's environmental policies was the establishment of the infrastructure to monitor and implement conservation initiatives. That infrastructure included agencies such as the Forest Service and the Inland Waterways Commission. Howland wrote *Theodore Roosevelt and His Times: A Chronicle of the Progressive Movement.*

T HE FIRST MESSAGE OF PRESIDENT ROOSEVELT TO CON- gress contained these words: "The forest and water problems are perhaps the most vital internal questions of the United States." At that moment, on December 3, 1901, the impulse was given that was to add to the American vocabulary two new words, "reclamation" and "conservation," that was to create two great constructive movements for the preservation, the increase, and the utilization of natural resources, and that was to establish a new relation-

Excerpted from *Theodore Roosevelt and His Times: A Chronicle of the Progressive Movement,* by Harold Howland (New Haven, CT: Yale University Press, 1921). Copyright © 1972 by Yale University Press. All rights reserved. Reprinted with permission.

ship on the part of the Federal Government to the nation's natural wealth.

Reclamation and conservation had this in common: the purpose of both was the intelligent and efficient utilization of the natural resources of the country for the benefit of the people of the country. But they differed in one respect, and with conspicuous practical effects. Reclamation, which meant the spending of public moneys to render fertile and usable arid lands hitherto deemed worthless, trod on no one's toes. It took from no one anything that he had; it interfered with no one's enjoyment of benefits which it was not in the public interest that he should continue to enjoy unchecked. It was therefore popular from the first, and the new policy went through Congress as though on well-oiled wheels. Only six months passed between its first statement in the Presidential message and its enactment into law. Conservation, on the other hand, had to begin by withholding the natural resources from exploitation and extravagant use. It had, first of all, to establish in the national mind the principle that the forests and mines of the nation are not an inexhaustible grab-bag into which whosoever will may thrust greedy and wasteful hands, and by this new understanding to stop the squandering of vast national resources until they could be economically developed and intelligently used. So it was inevitable that conservation should prove unpopular, while reclamation gained an easy popularity, and that those who had been feeding fat off the country's stores of forest and mineral wealth should oppose, with tooth and nail, the very suggestion of conservation.

Laying the Groundwork

It was on the first Sunday after he reached Washington as President, before he had moved into the White House, that Roosevelt discussed with two men, Gifford Pinchot and F.H. Newell, the twin policies that were to become two of the finest contributions to American progress of the Roosevelt Administrations. Both men were already in the Government service, both were men of broad vision and high constructive ability; with both Roosevelt had already worked when he was Governor of New York. The name of Newell, who became chief engineer of the Reclamation Service, ought to be better known popularly than it is in connection with the wonderful work that has been accomplished in making the desert lands of western America blossom and produce abundantly. The name of Pinchot, by a more fortunate combination of events, has become synonymous in the popular mind with the conservation movement.

On the very day that the first Roosevelt message was read to the Congress, a committee of Western Senators and Congressmen was organized, under the leadership of Senator Francis G. Newlands of Nevada, to prepare a Reclamation Bill. The only obstacle to the prompt enactment of the bill was the undue insistence upon State Rights by certain Congressmen, "who consistently fought for local and private interests as against the interests of the people as a whole." In spite of this shortsighted opposition, the bill became law on June 17, 1902, and the work of reclamation began without an instant's delay. The Reclamation Act set aside the proceeds of the sale of public lands for the purpose of reclaiming the waste areas of the arid West. Lands otherwise worthless were to be irrigated and in those new regions of agricultural productivity homes were to be established. The money so expended was to be repaid in due course by the settlers on the land and the sums repaid were to be used as a revolving fund for the continuous prosecution of the reclamation work. Nearly five million dollars was made immediately available for the work. Within four years, twenty-six "projects" had been approved by the Secretary of the Interior and work was well under way on practically all of them. They were situated in fourteen States—Arizona, Colorado, Idaho, Kansas, Montana, Nebraska, Washington,

Utah, Wyoming, New Mexico, North Dakota, Oregon, California, South Dakota. The individual projects were intended to irrigate areas of eight thousand to two hundred thousand acres each; and the grand total of arid lands to which water was thus to be brought by canals, tunnels, aqueducts, and ditches was more than a million and a half acres.

The work had to be carried out under the most difficult and adventurous conditions. The men of the Reclamation Service were in the truest sense pioneers, building great engineering works far from the railroads, where the very problem of living for the great numbers of workers required was no simple one. On the Shoshone in Wyoming these men built the highest dam in the world, 310 feet from base to crest. They pierced a mountain range in Colorado and carried the waters of the Gunnison River nearly six miles to the Uncompahgre Valley through a tunnel in the solid rock. The great Roosevelt dam on the Salt River in Arizona with its gigantic curved wall of masonry 280 feet high, created a lake with a capacity of fifty-six billion cubic feet, and watered in 1915 an area of 750,000 acres.

Boldness of Action

The work of these bold pioneers was made possible by the fearless backing which they received from the Administration at Washington. The President demanded of them certain definite results and gave them unquestioning support. In Roosevelt's own words, "the men in charge were given to understand that they must get into the water if they would learn to swim; and, furthermore, they learned to know that if they acted honestly, and boldly and fearlessly accepted responsibility, I would stand by them to the limit. In this, as in every other case, in the end the boldness of the action fully justified itself."

The work of reclamation was first prosecuted under the United States Geological Survey; but in the spring of 1908 the United States Reclamation Service was established to carry it on, under the direction of Mr. Newell, to whom the inception of the plan was due. Roosevelt paid a fine and well-deserved tribute to the man who originated and carried through this great national achievement when he said that "Newell's single-minded devotion to this great task, the constructive imagination which enabled him to conceive it, and the executive power and high character through which he and his assistant, Arthur P. Davis, built up a model service—all these made him a model servant. The final proof of his merit is supplied by the character and records of the men who later assailed him."

The assault to which Roosevelt thus refers was the inevitable aftermath of great accomplishment. Reclamation was popular, when it was proposed, while it was being carried out, and when the water began to flow in the ditches, making new lands of fertile abundance for settlers and farmers. But the reaction of unpopularity came the minute the beneficiaries had to begin to pay for the benefits received. Then arose a concerted movement for the repudiation of the obligation of the settlers to repay the Government for what had been spent to reclaim the land. The baser part of human nature always seeks a scapegoat; and it might naturally be expected that the repudiators and their supporters should concentrate their attacks upon the head of the Reclamation Service, to whose outstanding ability and continuous labor they owed that for which they were now unwilling to pay. But no attack, not even the adverse report of an ill-humored congressional committee, can alter the fact of the tremendous service that Newell and his loyal associates in the Reclamation Service did for the nation and the people of the United States. By 1915 reclamation had added to the arable land of the country a million and a quarter acres, of which nearly eight hundred thousand acres were already "under water," and largely under tillage, producing yearly more than eighteen million dollars' worth of crops.

Forests and Forestry

When Roosevelt became President there was a Bureau of Forestry in the Department of Agriculture, but it was a body entrusted with merely the study of forestry problems and principles. It contained all the trained foresters in the employ of the Government; but it had no public forest lands whatever to which the knowledge and skill of these men could be applied. All the forest reserves of that day were in the charge of the Public Land Office in the Department of the Interior. This was managed by clerks who knew nothing of forestry, and most, if not all, of whom had never seen a stick of the timber or an acre of the woodlands for which they were responsible. The mapping and description of the timber lay with the Geological Survey. So the national forests had no foresters and the Government foresters no forests.

It was a characteristic arrangement of the old days. More than that, it was a characteristic expression of the old attitude of thought and action on the part of the American people toward their natural resources. Dazzled and intoxicated by the inexhaustible riches of their bountiful land, they had concerned themselves only with the agreeable task of utilizing and consuming them. To their shortsighted vision there seemed always plenty more beyond. With the beginning of the twentieth century a prophet arose in the land to warn the people that the supply was not inexhaustible. He declared not only that the "plenty more beyond" had an end, but that the end was already in sight. This prophet was Gifford Pinchot. His warning went forth reinforced by all the authority of the Presidential office and all the conviction and driving power of the personality of Roosevelt himself. Pinchot's warning cry was startling:

> The growth of our forests is but one-third of the annual cut; and we have in store timber enough for only twenty or thirty years at our present rate of use. . . . Our

coal supplies are so far from being inexhaustible that if the increasing rate of consumption shown by the figures of the last seventy-five years continues to prevail, our supplies of anthracite coal will last but fifty years and of bituminous coal less than two hundred years. . . . Many oil and gas fields, as in Pennsylvania, West Virginia, and the Mississippi Valley, have already failed, yet vast quantities of gas continue to be poured into the air and great quantities of oil into the streams. Cases are known in which great volumes of oil were systematically burned in order to get rid of it. . . . In 1896, Professor Shaler, than whom no one has spoken with greater authority on this subject, estimated that in the upland regions of the States south of Pennsylvania, three thousand square miles of soil have been destroyed as the result of forest denudation, and that destruction was then proceeding at the rate of one hundred square miles of fertile soil per year. . . . The Mississippi River alone is estimated to transport yearly four hundred million tons of sediment, or about twice the amount of material to be excavated from the Panama Canal. This material is the most fertile portion of the richest fields, transformed from a blessing to a curse by unrestricted erosion. . . . The destruction of forage plants by overgrazing has resulted, in the opinion of men most capable of judging, in reducing the grazing value of the public lands by one-half.

The Proposal for Forest Lands

Here, then, was a problem of national significance, and it was one which the President attacked with his usual promptness and vigor. His first message to Congress called for the unification of the care of the forest lands of the public domain in a single body under the Department of Agriculture. He asked that legal authority be granted to the President to transfer to the Department of Agriculture lands for use as forest reserves. He declared that "the forest reserves should be set apart forever for the use and benefit of our people as a whole and not sacrificed to the short-sighted greed of a few." He supplemented this declaration with an explanation of the meaning and purpose of the forest policy which he urged should be adopted:

Wise forest protection does not mean the withdrawal of forest resources, whether of wood, water, or grass, from contributing their full share to the welfare of the people, but, on the contrary, gives the assurance of larger and more certain supplies. The fundamental idea of forestry is the perpetuation of forests by use. Forest protection is not an end in itself; it is a means to increase and sustain the resources of our country and the industries which depend upon them. The preservation of our forests is an imperative business necessity. We have come to see clearly that whatever destroys the forest, except to make way for agriculture, threatens our well-being.

The Forest Service Is Political Victory

Nevertheless it was four years before Congress could be brought to the common-sense policy of administering the forest lands still belonging to the Government. Pinchot and his associates in the Bureau of Forestry spent the interval profitably, however, in investigating and studying the whole problem of national forest resources and in drawing up enlightened and effective plans for their protection and development. Accordingly, when the act transferring the National Forests to the charge of the newly created United States Forest Service in the Department of Agriculture was passed early in 1905, they were ready for the responsibility.

The principles which they had formulated and which they now began to apply had been summed up by Roosevelt in the statement "that the rights of the public to the natural resources outweigh private rights and must be given the first consideration." Until the establishment of the Forest Service, private rights had almost always been allowed to overbalance public rights in matters that concerned not only the National Forests, but the public lands generally. It was the necessity of having this new principle recognized and adopted that made the way of the newly created Forest Service and of the whole Conservation movement so thorny. Those who had been used to making personal profit from free and unrestricted exploitation of the nation's natural resources would look only with antagonism on a movement which put a consideration of the general welfare first.

The Forest Service nevertheless put these principles immediately into practical application. The National Forests were opened to a regulated use of all their resources. A law was passed throwing open to settlement all land in the National Forests which was found to be chiefly valuable for agriculture. Hitherto all such land had been closed to the settler. Regulations were established and enforced which favored the settler rather than the large stockowner. It was provided that, when conditions required the reduction in the number of head of stock grazed in any National Forest, the vast herds of the wealthy owner should be affected before the few head of the small man, upon which the living of his family depended. The principle which excited the bitterest antagonism of all was the rule that any one, except a bona fide settler on the land, who took public property for private profit should pay for what he got. This was a new and most unpalatable idea to the big stock and sheep raisers, who had been accustomed to graze their animals at will on the richest lands of the public forests, with no one but themselves a penny the better off thereby. But the Attorney-General of the United States declared it legal to make the men who pastured their cattle and sheep in the National Forests pay for this privilege; and in the summer of 1906 such charges were for the first time made and collected. The trained foresters of the service were put in charge of the National Forests. As a result, improvement began to manifest itself in other ways. Within two years the fire prevention work alone had completely justified the new policy of forest regulation. Eighty-six per cent of the fires that did occur in the National Forests were held down to an area of five acres or less. The new service not only made rapid progress in saving the timber, but it began to make money for the nation by selling the timber. In 1905 the sales of timber brought in $60,000; three years later the return was $850,000.

The National Forests were trebled in size during the two Roosevelt Administrations with the result that there were 194,000,000 acres of publicly owned and administered forest lands when Roosevelt went out of office.

Roosevelt Built Support for Conservation by Linking It to American Values

Daniel O. Buehler

Theodore Roosevelt faced seemingly insurmountable obstacles in promoting his conservation initiatives. Not only was there little public support for the idea, but the notion of preserving nature would require a major ideological shift in the way natural resources were viewed. In order to accomplish his goals, the president linked the protection of natural resources with existing public beliefs and enduring American values of progress and liberty. In doing so Roosevelt was able to rally the public behind him, and conservation would become one of his enduring triumphs. At the time he wrote this, Daniel O. Buehler was completing his Ph.D. at the University of Maryland, where he studied communication.

IN 1908, AT THE GOVERNORS' CONFERENCE ON CONSERVA-tion, Theodore Roosevelt generated the necessary rhetorical intensity to set in motion a national conservation policy. Because conservation, as Roosevelt conceived it, was a novel policy, he confronted two rhetorical chal-

Excerpted from "Permanence and Change in Theodore Roosevelt's Conservation Jeremiad," by Daniel O. Buehler, *Western Journal of Communication*, Fall 1998. Copyright © 1998 by *Western Journal of Communication*. Reprinted with permission.

lenges in persuading his audience to accept his initiative. First, he had to create a sense of exigency. Second, he had to formulate a link between his policy and his audience's values and beliefs. To confront these challenges, Roosevelt turned to a subtly crafted jeremiad that presented the need for action and linked conservation with past values. . . .

A Land of Abundance

Settlers who came to the new world discovered a land that seemed to possess inexhaustible resources. Reports from the Lewis and Clark expedition revealed a fertile country harboring vast tracks of virgin forests, endless fields of grasslands, and enough precious minerals and wild animals to satisfy the most gluttonous desires. In his journal, William Clark recorded seeing "great numbers of Buffalow (sic), Elk, Deer, antilope (sic), beaver, Porcupins (sic), & water fowls . . . Geese, ducks of dif[ferent] kinds, & a flew (sic) Swan". John James Audubon's encounter with the passenger pigeon on a trip to Louisville is also revealing; he wrote, "The air was literally filled with Pigeons; the light of noon-day was obscured as by an eclipse". Given that the New World had what the old country had long lost— wilderness and its unlocked, overflowing treasure chest of untapped riches, many in the nineteenth century sought "to make a killing from . . . quickly extracting the cheap, virgin resources of the nation" [as stated by Samuel P. Hays].

For these new world settlers the wealth of natural resources was coupled with the belief that America was a land void of physical limitations and ecological thresholds. For example, on the Louisville trip, Audubon witnessed a collection of townspeople slaughter and feed on nothing but pigeons for over a week. Audubon responded to the event with simple amazement at the land's astonishing bounty of creatures. Thomas Jefferson ignored the issue of natural boundaries when he advised New World inhabitants to "go off in great numbers to search for vacant country" whenever they felt overcrowded or compressed. In a similar vein, St. John de Crevecoeur predicted, "Many ages will not see the shores of our great lakes replenished with inland nations, nor the unknown bounds of North America entirely peopled. Who can tell how far it extends?"

Operating under the myth of abundance, the yeoman farmer and unfettered pioneer heedlessly marched toward the Pacific Ocean, leaving behind a wake of depleted resources and an extraordinarily altered landscape. Henry David Thoreau complained that "nowadays almost all man's improvements, so called, as the building of houses, and the cutting down of the forest and of all large trees,

Roosevelt's Western Ways

H.W. Brands describes one of Roosevelt's early forays into conservation. As a rancher in the West, Roosevelt organized a stockmen's association in response to the problem of overgrazing on public lands.

His memory of the frontier code of justice would color Roosevelt's approach to international affairs, which were, in their own way, as lawless and anarchic as the affairs of the wild West. His Dakota days influenced his approach to domestic politics as well. Among other things, ranching made Roosevelt into a conservationist. The potential for overstocking the range weighed constantly on the minds of the ranchers of the plains. Had Roosevelt been content to run only those cattle that came with the Chimney Butte and Elkhorn ranches, no one would have bothered him; but when he moved to multiply their numbers by five or ten times, importing a thousand new head, the neighbors had to complain. Their complaints carried no force of law, however, because none of the complainants owned the land in question. . . . With minor exceptions, all grazed their herds

simply deform the landscape, and make it more and more tame and cheap". . . .

The Governors' Conference on Conservation

Alarmed by America's wasteful use of its natural resources, Theodore Roosevelt convened the first Governors' Conference on the 13th of May 1908, in an effort to awaken the nation to the "weightiest problem of [its] age . . . the adoption of measures for the conservation, development and judicious use of the natural resources of the country." Roosevelt opened the conference with a speech that set in motion the first comprehensive national policy concerning

on public land, to which no one west of Washington held legal title. On the open range it was first come, first served, a principle that invited abuse. Without putting the matter in so many words, all involved understood that they faced the dilemma of the commons, where each individual's pursuit of self-interest, in the form of grass for more of his cattle, threatened the ruin of all, in the form of degradation of the range and a massive dying off. Only by some concerted action, some self-denying compact, could the community avert the disaster. . . .

In other parts of the cattle country, ranchers had formed stockmen's associations to deal with overgrazing and other shared concerns; on his return to Dakota following the 1884 elections, Roosevelt set about creating just such an organization for the Little Missouri region. For weeks he rode from ranch to ranch talking up the need for a cattlemen's group. His canvassing paid off, and in mid-December the first meeting of the Little Missouri Stockmen's Association convened at Roberts Hall in Medora.

H.W. Brands, *T.R.: The Last Romantic.* New York: BasicBooks, 1997, pp. 185–88.

the conservation of natural resources. As Gifford Pinchot tells the story, Roosevelt's epochal policy of conservation was so well crafted that "it was instantly and universally accepted and approved by the people of the United States." In the estimation of one observer, "those present felt they were witnessing an important historical event. In its earnestness and restraint and suggestiveness it was perhaps the best speech Roosevelt ever made." Historian William Harbaugh notes that "throughout the nation [Roosevelt's] address was acclaimed as one of his greatest public utterances, perhaps the greatest". Stephen Fox asserts that beginning in 1908, "'conservation' was applied to everything that needed environmental protection" and eventually the "word passed into everyday language." Indeed, today launching the conservation movement is regarded as one of Roosevelt's most significant and constructive achievements.

As a result of the conference, thirty-six state conservation commissions were started, numerous scientific organizations created conservation committees, and a National Conservation Commission was established. In addition, conference participants authored and signed the landmark document, "Declaration of the Governors," which radically changed the federal-state relationship and openly declared the importance of conserving the nation's natural wealth for the benefit of "the People." In general, historians agree that Roosevelt's greatest contribution to the nation was the encouragement of conservation. As a testament to his legacy, in 1968, the National Wildlife Federation made Theodore Roosevelt the first inductee into its Conservation Hall of Fame.

Roosevelt's Challenges

Since conservation, as Roosevelt conceived it, was a novel policy, he confronted two rhetorical challenges in persuading his audience to accept his initiative. First, he had to create a sense of exigency, an urgency to resolve the environmental crisis. Second, he had to formulate a nexus between conservation and values and attitudes that his audience embraced. To negotiate these rhetorical challenges, Roosevelt turned to a subtly constructed jeremiad that presented the need for action and linked conservation with past values. . . .

Roosevelt's conservation speech offers a unique version of the jeremiad, one that does not chastise the public for breaking any particular moral covenant, but which nonetheless seeks to modify human behavior. For Roosevelt, America's great "sin" did not lie in individual citizens' failures to domesticate the landscape and advance civilization; rather, he felt America's great misdeed lay in the absence of a single, coherent plan that efficiently managed the nation's natural resources. Roosevelt's jeremiad made the American Dream's fidelity contingent on efficiently governing the country's consumptive behaviors. That is, instead of seeking individual atonement, Roosevelt sought to control the impulse of progress by systematically changing how the country managed its resources.

Although the jeremiad is always used as a call for change, the nature of that called-for change is significant: it always is a return to key values and beliefs. For example, African Americans utilized this aspect of the jeremiad in their calls for social change. As David Howard-Pitney explains, for African-Americans "the Black jeremiad became a powerful rhetorical tradition for denouncing every form of racial injustice as a betrayal of the American Dream.". . .

Similarly, Sacvan Bercovitch notes that leading feminists like Antoinette Brown Blackwell, Elizabeth Oakes Smith, and Elizabeth Cady Stanton also employed the familial jeremiadic formula when advocating women's rights. Like African-Americans, these feminists opposed the majority view, but they too appealed to principles valued by all Americans and aligned themselves with the American Dream in order to advance their cause. . . .

Crusading for Conservation

When Roosevelt became President in 1901, he altered conservation's status by making it one of his administration's defining characteristics. To do so, Roosevelt carried on an unprecedented media campaign that spotlighted conservation. He staged presidential events that were intended to draw press coverage of conservation issues, he prepared speeches and statements for public consumption on conservation, and he provided occasional leaks about conservation matters to the press that were designed to undermine congressional opponents. The White House Governors' Conference on Conservation in 1908 marked a high point in Roosevelt's media campaign. Throughout his campaign, as Leroy Dorsey has noted, Roosevelt rhetorically manipulated key elements of the frontier myth while promulgating conservation. As a result, Roosevelt both educated the public on the social and moral virtues associated with conservation and urged the public to pressure Congress to accept some of his policy proposals.

In addition to his media campaign, Roosevelt accomplished numerous noteworthy conservation projects while in office through the use of his veto and executive power. For instance, he created the Inland Waterways Commission to efficiently and effectively manage the nation's water resources. He started the National Country Life Commission in the hope of improving the farmer's quality of life and crop production. He tripled the federal forest reserves from approximately 50 million acres to nearly 150 million acres, established five national parks, sixteen national monuments, and fifty-one wildlife refuges.

Despite crusading energetically for conservation, Roosevelt failed to establish a unified conservation policy because of a lack of bureaucratic unity and an unsupportive Republican Congress. By 1905, the newly created Forest Service and twenty other government agencies all were practicing conservation, but with little knowledge of each others' activities. No common ground was sought among the agencies: no cross-fertilization of conservation ideas were entertained, no cooperative efforts were being made to pull resources together and implement joint programs. Instead, bureau chiefs operated solely within their own agencies while simultaneously battling with each other over funds, jurisdiction, credit, and influence. Conspicuously lacking was a conservation policy that fused the agencies together and induced them to work for a common purpose.

Political Strategies

Politically, Roosevelt's conservation program and his efforts to moderate the exploitation of natural resources were consistently challenged by Congress, ranchers, mine operators, loggers, power companies, and the Western states. For instance, in 1907, Congress attached an amendment to the Agricultural Appropriations Bill that effectively prohibited the President from creating additional forest reserves. Vetoing the bill would have seriously hindered the Agricultural Department's and Forest Service's conservation activities. So, Roosevelt left the bill sitting on his desk, while he quickly used his executive power to add 16 million acres of forests, mineral deposits, and power sites to the forest reserves. Roosevelt eventually signed the bill, but not before creating or increasing the size of thirty-two forest reserves. Although furious, Congress was helpless to do anything. However, when Roosevelt subsequently sought funding for the Inland Waterways Commission and National Country Life Commission, Congress refused to allocate operating funds to these Commissions. In general, Congress treated the President's proposals with diminishing respect over time.

Roosevelt's lack of success in gaining congressional support for a unified conservation policy also stemmed from conservation's apparent challenge to fundamental beliefs, and private properly rights in particular. At the time, it was generally believed that "ownership and management of land ought to be left entirely in the hands of ordinary individuals, acting informally among themselves" [according to Donald Worster]. De Crevecoeur expressed this attitude when he declared, "The instant I enter

Roosevelt successfully built support for conservation by linking it to the American concepts of progress and liberty.

on my own land, the bright idea of property, of exclusive right, of independence exalt my mind." He went on to say that "this formally rude soil . . . has established all our rights; on it is founded our rank, our freedom, our power as citizens, our importance as inhabitants of such a distinct place". By placing the management of public lands in the hands of the federal government, conservation threatened the right to private property.

Roosevelt realized that if he wanted conservation to be an enduring part of his administration's legacy, he needed to make it politically salient and to elevate it to a general reform movement, one that could be linked to socially valued ideas and beliefs. To do so, Roosevelt crafted a rhetorical situation that enabled him to give conservation a much needed unified vision and national flavor. Cognizant that conservation's future rested with the states and not solely with Congress, Roosevelt gathered together a remarkable group of regional opinion leaders for an unprecedented meeting. This Conference brought together for the first time the Governors of the states and territories, numerous influential Senators and Representatives, all the Supreme Court Justices, and noteworthy public figures including William Jennings Bryan, Andrew Carnegie, and James J. Hill with conservation as the conference topic. All this manipulation was done with one objective in mind—to convince the audience that protection, preservation, and wise use of the country's natural resources should be dealth with as one great common problem involving collective action at both state and national levels. . . .

Invoking History

Roosevelt began his address to the Governors' Conference by evoking the nation's epic history and advancing a theme of progress that linked America's rise to prominence with nature. The President proclaimed,

Nature has supplied to us in the United States . . . more kinds of resources in a more lavish degree than has ever been the case at any other time with any other people. Our position in the world has been attained by the extent and thoroughness of the control we have achieved over nature.

Roosevelt then drove this point home by taking stock of the nation's prosperity:

The discovery and utilization of mineral fuels and alloys have given us the lead over all other nations in the production of steel. The discovery and utilization of coal and iron have given us our railways, and have led to such industrial development as has never before been seen. The vast wealth of lumber in our forests, the riches of our soils and mines, the discovery of gold and mineral oils, combined with the efficiency of our transportation, have made the condition of our life unparalleled in comfort and convenience.

Roosevelt based his historical assessment on the wisdom of the country's founding fathers and their reason for creating the Constitution. He stated,

Washington clearly saw that the perpetuity of the States could only be secured by union, and that the only feasible basis of union was an economic one, in other words, that it must be based on the development and use of their natural resources.

It followed, according to Roosevelt, that "the Constitution of the United States thus grew in large part out of the necessity for united action in the wise use of one of our natural resources."

Roosevelt's ingenious appropriation of the jeremiad allowed him to evoke a particular conception of America's past, one that accounted for the country's prosperity; and also generated and attributed social meaning to a form of behavior that previously had gone unnoticed. Roosevelt claimed, "It is safe to say that the prosperity of our people depends directly on the energy and intelligence with which our natural resources are used. It is equally clear that these resources are the final basis of national power and perpetuity." By highlighting the fact that America's impressive status is due largely to the country's ability to wisely manage its natural resources, Roosevelt converted the process of civilizing the land into a subject for critique. In doing so, Roosevelt performed an important task generally fulfilled by movement spokespersons: he transformed a once-innocuous behavior into something intolerable. His history of the country's formidable growth provided a smooth segue into the "great material question of today."

While he was establishing the exigency and introducing conservation as the solution, Roosevelt also melded his policy with forces of the past. . . . In its basic form, Roosevelt's conservation policy involved moving away from a governmental laissez-faire approach to public land management and toward centralization via efficient governmental control of natural resources. Roosevelt used the jeremiad rhetorically to construct a bridge between the past laissez-faire policy and his radical unified conservation policy by articulating a vision of a victorious future based on the sustenance of traditional values. Roosevelt rendered his policy credible to the public and affirmed core American values and beliefs by weaving together conservation and these conventional American ideas: humans hold dominion over nature so long as they perform their role as land stewards; the American Dream is contingent on progress and economic growth; and the frontier is a provider of economic and political liberty.

Roosevelt's jeremiad maintained the cultural mythology that humans hold dominion over nature by tactfully heralding conservation's ability not only to manage nature efficiently, but actually to improve its productivity. Early evidence for the idea that humans dominate nature is readily found in the Biblical book of Genesis which avers that God placed man (sic) in the earthly garden to "guard and keep it." Roosevelt's extensive account of the country's rise to prominence reinforced this human over nature hierarchy and tapped into America's pride in conquering the wilderness. Failure to further dominate nature and possibly to relapse back into a state of chaos would be a devastating blow to America's ethos and would nullify the belief in its dominion. To secure the country's ethos, Roosevelt offered the nation a policy that would bolster its superiority and power over nature—conservation.

Roosevelt Redefined the Frontier Myth to Build Support for Conservation

Leroy G. Dorsey

Roosevelt's impact on the environment was especially dramatic because he managed to change the view that many Americans had of the nation's natural resources. Leroy G. Dorsey asserts that many people in the United States viewed the country's environment as a collection of resources or tools that existed mainly for human use. In order to increase public support for conservation, according to Dorsey, Roosevelt redefined the image of the frontier hero from one who was violent and exploitative to one who was a caretaker of the environment. He also utilized his "bully pulpit" and impressive oratory to outwit his political opponents in Congress on the issue. Dorsey is a professor of speech communication at Texas A&M University.

A S THE TWENTIETH CENTURY OPENED, THE PRESIDENCY shifted much of its emphasis from that of an administrative office to more of a bully pulpit. The presidency can now best be characterized as a rhetorical institution, one that reflects Richard Neustadt's axiom that "presidential power is the power to persuade." According to James

Excerpted from "The Frontier Myth in Presidential Rhetoric: Theodore Roosevelt's Campaign for Conservation," by Leroy G. Dorsey, *Western Journal of Communication*, Winter 1995. Copyright © 1995 by *Western Journal of Communication*. Reprinted with permission.

Ceaser, Glen Thurow, Jeffrey Tulis, and Joseph Bessette, the "rhetorical presidency" describes a chief executive who employs oratory not only to motivate the public into pressuring Congress to support a legislative agenda, but also to provide moral leadership for the nation.

Faced with an increasingly diverse public and the technology to reach it, modern presidents have sought the means to communicate with the nation in a common yet provocative language. Thus, some chief executives have turned to storytelling. Under this model of rhetorical leadership, presidents may relate stories that feature intriguing characters engaged in epic adventures in an equally fantastic realm. These myths, when merged with stories about "real" peoples' experiences, can act as compelling symbols which the president can use to shape the audience's identity and to prescribe its social behaviors

The Frontier Myth, in particular, has been a much used story by several rhetorical presidents to inspire audiences and to energize policies. Briefly, the Myth offers an account of how the constant challenge of an unknown and limitless frontier turns some individuals into martial heroes who, because of their epic struggles, come to symbolize American values such as progress and prosperity. . . .

Theodore Roosevelt . . . rhetorically used the Frontier Myth. . . . However, . . . rather than employ the Myth in a traditional sense to promote a martial or economic policy, Roosevelt linked it to the notion of conservation. In the process, he radically altered the key elements of the Myth to accommodate and to promote the preservation of the environment. . . .

Specifically, Roosevelt altered the traditional Frontier Myth in three major ways. First, he recast the hero's role in the Frontier Myth by replacing the Myth's traditional hero, whose relationship to the frontier had been violent and exploitative, with the yeoman farmer-hero, whose wise use of the environment protected it. Second, Roosevelt sought to redefine the "unlimited" frontier. To that end, he linked certain businesses' decreasing economic opportunities to the "finite" nature of the environment. In addition, he argued that while limited, the frontier provided the more valuable opportunity of spiritual regeneration. Finally, Roosevelt redefined the value of "progress" in the frontier narrative to accommodate his revised versions of the hero and the frontier. As a result, progress represented the conservation of nature through common effort rather than by the exploitation of the environment by individuals. By these three moves, Roosevelt promoted a substantial redefinition of the relationship between the Frontier Myth and the American people. . . .

Theodore Roosevelt apparently believed that the reduction of America's sacred history to that of a conqueror-hero of an unlimited frontier-universe had brought about severe environmental concerns. As he remarked in his "First Annual Message," the conservation of the land, forest, water, and animals represented "the most vital internal questions of the United States." When he succeeded President McKinley in 1901, Roosevelt saw the environment under siege. At the time, one-half of the country's timber had been cut, with the annual use rate at four times the new growth rate. Furthermore, 200 million acres of forest land had been destroyed with over a billion tons of topsoil washed away. Wasteful mining methods wreaked havoc as well. Not only did they garner four billion tons of coal, but they also destroyed or made inaccessible an equal quantity. Finally, animals such as the heath hen, buffalo, fur seal, passenger pigeon, alligator, elk, bear, and bighorn sheep were either wiped out or neared extinction due to profit-minded hunters.

President Roosevelt attempted a revolutionary alteration of the Frontier Myth icons to promote conservation. Consistent with his rhetorical conception of the presidency, he went to the public with a revised Frontier Myth, one that glorified a preserver-hero who acted within a finite, frontier-universe. To disseminate these new mythic elements to the widest audience, Roosevelt not only incorporated them in his addresses from the White House, but he also revolutionized the use of the speaking tour. He gave "swings around the circle," which were even then derided as hackneyed publicity devices, a new sense of purpose and flair. Like later rhetorical presidents, Roosevelt frequently stumped across the country as the nation's preeminent storyteller, using the media to retell his revised versions of the frontier hero and environmental universe. Furthermore, in his Governors' Conference address in 1908, he adapted the third element of the Frontier Myth, the narrative, to accommodate the altered icons of the hero and universe. In that speech he redefined progress in America's covenant so as to provide a new purpose for the country in relation to the environment.

The Farmer as Hero

According to David Noble, the yeoman farmer had long been a "figure of superior virtue" in the minds of the American people. By the 1890s, however, the myth of the farmer-hero had been "seriously undermined." The decline in the farmer's image, Noble writes, was due in part to the rise of the city as the primary dwelling place as well as to the "realistic descriptions of the heavy burden of farm work . . . the loneliness of farm life, the dependence of cruelly capricious weather, and the endless financial problems of the farmer". But more than that, the myth of the farmer who used the land in productive ways seemed timid and uninspiring in comparison to the romanticized figure of the Frontier Myth's new heroic icon: the Old West cowboy. By the turn of the century, the cowboy's vices of rootlessness and lawlessness on the frontier had been transformed into virtues, while the "sodbuster" seemed by comparison to lack those American values of courage and adventure.

This ascendance of the rebellious cowboy and the continuation of the conqueror-hero icon apparently disturbed Roosevelt. As a result, he attempted to buck this trend. A noted rancher, hunter, and naturalist himself, Roosevelt's love of nature promoted a keen sensitivity to the environment and a disdain for those people whose actions threatened it. For example, despite his zeal for hunting, Roosevelt differentiated between hunting to embrace the frontier experience and hunting for the purpose of economic profit; for him, the latter represented wholesale slaughter with inevitable extinction while the former did not. As a result, he had long resisted celebrating the destructiveness of the Frontier Myth's traditional hero. In his works prior to the presidency, most notably *The Winning of the West,* Roosevelt had lionized instead the productive backwoods farmers, crediting them with estimable qualities such as great physical strength, iron resolve, and a strong moral sense.

Roosevelt endorsed the modern yeoman farmers as the true heroes of the Frontier Myth. According to the President, they exhibited the heroic traits of American greatness. It was the farmers, he asserted before a 1902 audience in Maine, "more than any other of our citizens to-day, [that are] called upon continually to exercise the qualities which we like to think of as typical of the United States . . . the qualities of rugged independence, masterful resolution, individual energy, and resourcefulness." Again in his "Sixth Annual Message," Roosevelt likened the contemporary farmer to the traditional frontier heroes. The former, like the latter, were rugged individualists since they "must primarily do most for themselves." Such traditional characteristics as moral resolve and physical strength, Roosevelt declared at a 1907 celebration for the founding of agricultural colleges, were exhibited by contemporary farmers and accounted for their success: "no government aid or direction can take the place of a strong and upright character; of goodness of heart combined with clearness of head, and that strength and toughness of fibre necessary to wring success from a rough workaday world."

Roosevelt's celebratory vision of the contemporary yeoman farmer essentially borrowed the ethos of those mythic frontier farmers who had played a central role in America's sacred history. For example, during a 1903 address in South Dakota, Roosevelt likened the contemporary farmer to those who first built the nation:

> the farmer himself still retains, because of his surrounding and the nature of his work, to a pre-eminent degree the qualities which we like to think of as distinctly American in considering our early history. The man who tills his own farm . . . still exists more nearly under the conditions which obtained when the 'embattled farmers' of '76 made this country a nation than is true of any others of our people.

A Symbol for the Nation

Roosevelt illustrated this point again four years later in his "Seventh Annual Message." "We began our existence as a nation of farmers," he stated, "and in every great crisis of the past a peculiar dependence has had to be placed upon the farming population; and this dependence has hitherto been justified." Now was not the time, Roosevelt charged, for this icon of American culture to be discarded.

Roosevelt believed that what the country needed was not the frontier-conqueror icon of times past, presently incarnated as the lawless cowboy, but the restoration of an American hero that could symbolize the conservation of the nation's resources. Rather than emulate the traditional conqueror-hero of the Frontier Myth who had "but one thought about a tree, and that was to cut it down," Roosevelt declared to the Forest Congress in 1905 that the country needed a symbol that would act as a gatekeeper to

America's natural wealth The frontier figure that Roosevelt charged with providing this example, and through whom the audience could vicariously identify, was the yeoman farmer. According to him, the country needed to recognize that farmers' wise use of the environment formed "the basis of all the other achievements of the American people."

Roosevelt recast the heroic icon of the frontier, calling for a protagonist who embraced the wise use of the environment. As he observed during a 1903 "Address at San Luis Obispo, California," the nation should not revere the people "whose aim it is merely to skin the soil and go on; to skin the country, to take off the timber, to exhaust it, and go on." For too long, he decided in his "Seventh Annual Message," too many people had ignored the fact that failing to conserve the environment constituted "the fundamental problem which underlies almost every other problem in our national life." He asserted that the contemporary farmer provided a practical lesson to the country. Instead of exploiting and ruining the land like certain miners and lumber operators, farmers worked to conserve nature's resources. As Roosevelt stated in his "Eight Annual Message," farmers epitomized the conservationist spirit just as their predecessor did: "a farmer, after all his life making his living from his farm, will, if he is an expert farmer, leave it as an asset of increased value to his son, so we should leave our national domain to our children, increased in value and not worn out."

Farmers who conserved nature's resources through their wise use of them promoted the permanent interests of the country. Just as mythical heroes struggled for a greater good, such as cooperating with the community for its protection, so too did contemporary farmers protect civilization by preserving its resources. Roosevelt told a 1903 Stanford University crowd that it should applaud the farmer as a person "who comes in not to take what he can out of the soil and leave, having exploited the country, but who comes to dwell therein, to bring up his children and to leave them the heritage in the country not merely unimpaired, but if possible even improved." For Roosevelt, the farmer-hero epitomized the conservationist who would use the water, forests, and land "so that by the very fact of the use they will become more valuable as possessions."

Although he replaced the traditional Frontier Myth's hero, Roosevelt's version still reflected the established Myth's familiar and compelling paradox between acting alone and cooperating with a group. The modern farmer-heroes resembled their original counterparts in that they manifested the traditional characteristics of the latter, most notably the trait of rugged individualism. And in order to meet their "goodness" requirement, Roosevelt maintained that these modern heroes opted to protect the community by working to safeguard the environment.

The Finite Frontier

As an icon abstracted from America's sacred history, the frontier had been seen primarily as an unlimited expanse with as many opportunities. However, most of the opportunities afforded by the Myth had reduced the frontier to a source of profit, a commodity to be bought and sold in the marketplace. The frontier's "beauty is associated with riches," [writer Jenni] Calder notes, "rolling grass lands mean cattle" and "mountains mean gold initially, then later silver, copper and lead." Roosevelt attempted to alter these perceptions of the frontier-universe. In seeking to make the frontier a limited object, he linked its finite nature to the economic opportunities of his audience. Furthermore, he downplayed the capitalistic aspect of the frontier in order to promote its spiritual dimension.

Roosevelt acknowledged the economic necessity of the frontier. According to him, the government's conservation policies would help to ensure the fiscal prosperity of the nation. For example, he stated in his "First Annual Message" that federal laws protecting certain forested areas were not an end in themselves: "it is a means to increase and sustain the resources of our country and the industries which depend upon them." "The preservation of our forests," he granted, was "an imperative business necessity."

However, to act as if there was an unlimited source of frontier-capital, Roosevelt maintained, was reprehensible. On this point, he blamed a human evil in the form of certain private business interests. Unlike the traditional Frontier Myth which featured a primarily "scenic" menace, the President's rhetoric broke with that tradition and identified deliberate, malicious human agents that calculatingly exploited the nation's resources. In particular, Roosevelt depicted the timber barons as little more than reckless looters. In a 1905 Washington, D.C. address, for example, he alleged that loggers had brought the nation to the verge of a timber famine. "The individual whose idea of developing the country is to cut every stick of timber off of it and then leave a barren desert," he warned, was a "curse and not a blessing to the country." Two years later he echoed that charge in his "Seventh Annual Message":

> There are persons who find it to their immense pecuniary benefit to destroy the forests by lumbering. . . . A big lumbering company, impatient for immediate returns and not caring to look far enough ahead, will often deliberately destroy all the good timber in a region, hoping afterward to move on to some new country.

These people, Roosevelt concluded in his "Eighth Annual Message," deliberately engaged in immoral behavior for the sole purpose of purchasing "a little gain for themselves."

A New View of Forests

Roosevelt played on the fears of those industries that engaged in exploitative practices against the environment by predicting their eventual economic misfortune. Speaking before the Forest Congress in 1905, he warned that for too long forests had been considered obstacles to be cleared. The forests were not limitless, Roosevelt maintained, and it remained only a matter of time before many industries suffered the consequences of a timber famine. He asserted that "unless the forests of the United States can be made ready to meet the vast demands which [this nation's] growth will inevitably bring, commercial disaster . . . is inevitable." Roosevelt reminded the audience that not only the loggers would suffer since "the railroads must have ties," "the miner must have timber," and "the stockman must have fence posts." The greed of a few business interests would affect any industry that was "dependent upon the existence of permanent and suitable supplies" from the forests.

But for Roosevelt, conserving the frontier provided more than just an economic benefit to the country. Conservation represented the means to regenerate the American spirit. As a rhetorical president, Roosevelt attempted to elevate the audience's concern beyond material matters to remind it of the sacred power of the frontier.

While the limitless frontier had long since disappeared, Roosevelt maintained, it was imperative that at least small pockets of wilderness be preserved. These pockets helped to maintain Americans' physical vigor. The forest reserves, he stated in his "First Annual Message," afforded "free camping grounds for the ever-increasing numbers of men and women who have learned to find rest [and] health in the splendid forests and flower-clad meadows of our mountains." During a tour of the western states in 1903, he asserted that the national parks he established would allow Americans to restore their physical prowess, just as their pioneer ancestors had likewise been transformed. At the gateway to Yellowstone National Park, he assured his audience that conservationists "will be able to ensure to themselves and to their children and to their children's children much of the old-time pleasure of the hardy life of the wilderness and of the hunter in the wilderness." These wilderness refuges, these sanctuaries of the mythologized western lands, still provided the conditions that could spur the "love of adventure" and the "hardihood to take advantage of it."

Despite the limited size of the frontier, Roosevelt believed in its mystical dimension and promoted its power to resuscitate the flagging spiritual nature of the American people. In a larger sense, Roosevelt's rhetoric linked the natural wonder of these isolated frontier areas to a Creator, reestablishing this icon's supernatural quality. During his 1903 visit to California, Roosevelt spoke reverentially about nature and its effect on those who experienced it: "lying out at night under those giant Sequoias was lying in a temple built by no hand of man, a temple grander than any human architect could by any possibility build." For Roosevelt, safeguarding nature's majesty went beyond any practical concerns, as he declared before another California audience:

> Yesterday I saw for the first time a grove of your great trees, a grove which it has taken the ages several thousands of years to build up; and I feel most emphatically that we should not turn a tree which was old when the first Egyptian conqueror penetrated to the valley of the Euphrates . . . into shingles. That, you may say, is not looking at the matter from the practical standpoint. There is nothing more practical in the end than the preservation of beauty, than the preservation of anything that appeals to the higher emotions in mankind.

The conservation of America's wilderness, then, became the practical application of Roosevelt's vision of a great nation. Not only would conservation provide the country's commercial foundation but, equally important, it would also act as an antidote to spiritual malaise in the modern world.

CHAPTER
2

REGULATING
BUSINESS AND
BUSTING TRUSTS

Roosevelt Staked Out a Middle Ground on Trusts

Harold Howland

During Roosevelt's presidency, public opinion in the United States was strongly divided about the role and influence of trusts and monopolies. Many people believed that trusts were good for the economy because they increased the efficiency of companies. On the other hand, many felt that trusts and monopolies limited competition and caused price inflation. Harold Howland contends that Roosevelt adopted a unique "middle ground" that protected consumers while allowing some trusts and monopolies to continue. As such, Roosevelt was not the avid antimonopolist that many historians portrayed him to be. Instead, he was a politician forced to make pragmatic decisions and was far more pro-business than most people perceived. Howland is the author of *Theodore Roosevelt and His Times: A Chronicle of the Progressive Movement.*

D URING THE TIMES OF ROOSEVELT, THE AMERICAN PEOPLE were profoundly concerned with the trust problem. So was Roosevelt himself. In this important field of the relations between "big business" and the people he had a perfectly definite point of view, though he did not have a cut and dried programme. He was always more interested in a point of view than in a programme, for he realized that the one is lasting, the other shifting. He knew that if you stand on sound footing and look at a subject from the true angle, you may safely modify your plan of action as often and as rapidly as may be necessary to fit changing conditions. But if your footing is insecure or your angle of vision distorted, the most attractive programme in the world may come to ignominious disaster.

There were, broadly speaking, three attitudes toward the trust problem which were strongly held by different groups in the United States. At one extreme was the threatening growl of big business, "Let us alone!" At the other pole was the shrill outcry of William Jennings Bryan and his fellow exhorters, "Smash the trusts!" In the golden middle ground was the vigorous demand of Roosevelt for a "square deal."

The Need for Something New

In his first message to Congress, the President set forth his point of view with frankness and clarity. His comprehensive discussion of the matter may be summarized thus: The tremendous and highly complex industrial development which went on with great rapidity during the latter half of the nineteenth century produced serious social problems. The old laws and the old customs which had almost the binding force of law were once quite sufficient to regulate the accumulation and distribution of wealth. Since the industrial changes which have so enormously increased the productive power of mankind, these regulations are no longer sufficient. The process of the creation of great corporate fortunes has aroused much antagonism; but much of this antagonism has been without warrant. There have been, it is true, abuses connected with the accumulation of wealth; yet no fortune can be accumulated in legitimate business except by conferring immense incidental benefits upon others. The men who have driven the great railways across the continent, who have built up commerce and developed manufactures, have on the whole done great good to the people at large. Without such men the material development of which Americans are so justly proud never could have taken place. They should therefore recognize the immense importance of this material development by leaving as unhampered as is compatible with the public good the strong men upon whom the success of business inevitably rests. It cannot too often be pointed out that to strike with ignorant violence at the interests of one set of men almost inevitably endangers the interests of all. The fundamental rule in American national life is that, on the whole and in the long run, we shall all go up or down together. Many of those who have made it their vocation to denounce the great industrial combinations appeal especially to the primitive instincts of hatred and fear. These are precisely the two emotions which unfit men for cool and steady judgment. The whole history of the world shows that legislation, in facing new industrial conditions, will generally be both unwise and ineffective unless it is undertaken only after calm inquiry and with sober self-restraint.

Justice for Two Sides

This is one side of the picture as it was presented by the President in his message to Congress. It was characteristic that this aspect should be put first, for Roosevelt always insisted upon doing justice to the other side before he demanded justice for his own. But he then proceeded to set forth the other side with equal vigor: There is a widespread conviction in the minds of the American people that the great corporations are in certain of their features and tendencies hurtful to the general welfare. It is true that real and grave evils have arisen, one of the chief of them being overcapitalization, with its many baleful consequences. This state of affairs demands that combination and concentration in business should be, not prohibited, but supervised and controlled. Corporations engaged in interstate commerce should be regulated if they are found to exercise a license working to the public injury. The first essential in determining how to deal with the great industrial combinations is knowledge of the facts. This is to be obtained only through publicity, which is the one sure remedy we can now invoke before it can be determined what further remedies are needed. Corporations should be subject to proper governmental supervision, and full and accurate information as to their operations should be made public at regular intervals. The nation should assume powers of supervision and regulation over all corporations doing an interstate business. This is especially true where the corporation derives a portion of its wealth from the existence of some monopolistic element or tendency in its business. The Federal Government should regulate the activities of corporations doing an interstate business, just as it regulates the activities of national banks, and, through the Interstate Commerce Commission, the operations of the railroads.

Roosevelt was destined, however, not to achieve the full measure of national control of corporations that he desired. The elements opposed to his view were too powerful. There was a fortuitous involuntary partnership—though it was not admitted and was even violently denied—between the advocates of "Let us alone!" and of "Smash the trusts!" against the champion of the middle way. . . .

Addressing the Problem

When Roosevelt became President, there were three directions in which energy needed to be applied to the solution of the trust problem: in the more vigorous enforcement of the laws already on the statute books; in the enactment of necessary new laws on various phases of the subject; and in the arousing of an intelligent and militant public opinion in relation to the whole question. To each of these purposes the

Balancing Competing Interests

Arthur M. Johnson, a scholar who has published articles on Theodore Roosevelt, points out how the president sought to address the public pressure to regulate big business without harming the economy or losing the political support of business leaders.

Shifting responsibility for dealing with the antitrust problem was no answer to the mounting public pressures for affirmative action to use the [Sherman Anti-Trust] statute as a counterforce to the combination movement, and Theodore Roosevelt, as McKinley's successor, accepted this fact. Like McKinley, however, Roosevelt had no desire to antagonize the big businessmen whose support was essential to his personal political ambitions. Furthermore, his own inclination was to accept large-scale enterprise as a basically desirable development for the nation's economy. The problem for Roosevelt, then, resolved itself into one of choosing the means that would give the Sherman Act meaning without thereby basically altering the structure that big business had given to the economy. If success attended these efforts, the power of the federal government over business would be vindicated to the satisfaction of the electorate without the alienation of big businessmen from Theodore Roosevelt and the Republican party.

Arthur M. Johnson, "Antitrust Policy in Transition, 1908: Ideal and Reality," *The Mississippi Valley Historical Review*, vol. 48, no. 3, December 1961, pp. 415–34.

new President applied himself with characteristic vigor.

The Sherman Anti-Trust law, which had already been on the Federal statute books for eleven years, forbade "combinations in restraint of trade" in the field of interstate commerce. During three administrations, eighteen actions had been brought by the Government for its enforcement. At the opening of the twentieth century it was a grave question whether the Sherman law was of any real efficacy in preventing the evils that arose from unregulated combination in business. A decision of the United States Supreme Court, rendered in 1895 in the so-called Knight case, against the American Sugar Refining Company, had, in the general belief, taken the teeth out of the Sherman law. In the words of Mr. [William Howard] Taft,

> The effect of the decision in the Knight case upon the popular mind, and indeed upon Congress as well, was to discourage hope that the statute could be used to accomplish its manifest purpose and curb the great industrial trusts which, by the acquisition of all or a large percentage of the plants engaged in the manufacture of a commodity, by the dismantling of some and regulating the output of others, were making every effort to restrict production, control prices, and monopolize the business.

It was obviously necessary that the Sherman act, unless it were to pass into innocuous desuetude, should have the original vigor intended by Congress restored to it by a new interpretation of the law on the part of the Supreme Court. Fortunately an opportunity for such a change presented itself with promptness. A small group of powerful financiers had arranged to take control of practically the entire system of railways in the Northwest, "possibly," Roosevelt has said, "as the first step toward controlling the entire railway system of the country." They had brought this about by organizing the Northern Securities Company to hold the majority of the stock of two competing railways, the Great Northern and the Northern Pacific. At the direction of President Roosevelt, suit was brought by the Government to prevent the merger. The defendants relied for protection upon the immunity afforded by the decision in the Knight case. But the Supreme Court now took more advanced ground, decreed that the Northern Securities Company was an illegal combination, and ordered its dissolution.

A Tool for Trust-Busting

By the successful prosecution of this case the Sherman act was made once more a potentially valuable instrument for the prevention of the more flagrant evils that flow from "combinations in restraint of trade." During the remaining years of the Roosevelt Administrations, this legal instrument was used with aggressive force for the purpose for which it was intended. In seven years and a half, forty-four prosecutions were brought under it by the Government, as compared with eighteen in the preceding eleven years. The two most famous trust cases, next to the Northern Securities case and even surpassing it in popular interest, because of the stupendous size of the corporations involved, were those against the Standard Oil Company and the American Tobacco Company. These companion cases were not finally decided in the Supreme Court until the Administration of President Taft; but their prosecution was begun while Roosevelt was in office and by his direction. They were therefore a definite part of his campaign for the solution of the vexed trust problem. Both cases were decided, by every court through which they passed, in favor of the Government. The Supreme Court finally in 1911 decreed that both the Standard Oil and the Tobacco trusts were in violation of the Sherman act and ordered their dissolution. There could now no longer be any question that the Government could in fact exercise its sovereign will over even the greatest and the most powerful of modern business organizations. . . .

But the proving of the anti-trust law as an effective weapon against the flagrantly offending trusts, according to Roosevelt's conviction, was only a part of the battle. As he said, "monopolies can, although in rather cumbrous fashion, be broken up by lawsuits. Great business combinations, however, cannot possibly be made useful instead of noxious industrial agencies merely by lawsuits, and especially by lawsuits supposed to be carried on for their destruction and not for their control and regulation." He took, as usual, the constructive point of view. He saw both sides of the trust question—the inevitability and the beneficence of combination in modern business, and the danger to the public good that lay in the unregulated and uncontrolled wielding of great power by private individuals. He believed that the thing to do with great power was not to destroy it but to use it, not to forbid its acquisition but to direct its application. So he set himself to the task of securing fresh legislation regarding the regulation of corporate activities.

Such legislation was not easy to get; for the forces of reaction were strong in Congress. But several significant steps in this direction were taken before Roosevelt went out of office. The new Federal Department of Commerce and Labor was created, and its head became a member of the Cabinet. The Bureau of Corporations was established in the same department. These new executive agencies were given no regulatory powers, but they did perform excellent service in that field of publicity on the value of which Roosevelt laid so much stress.

Roosevelt Increased Government Involvement in Business and Labor

George E. Mowry

In his economic policies, Theodore Roosevelt endeavored to balance the interests of large businesses and the nation's consumers and workers. Soon after entering office, he took action against the Northern Securities Company. This was the first in a long line of antitrust or antimonopoly measures. Concurrently, Roosevelt undertook action to help end a coal miner strike. George E. Mowry writes that the young president's actions were instrumental in reducing the power and influence of big business in the United States and establishing the federal government as a legitimate arbitrator between workers and employers. Mowry is the author of *The Era of Theodore Roosevelt, 1900–1912*.

O N FEBRUARY 19, 1902, THE ATTORNEY GENERAL, PHIlander C. Knox, startled the country and threw the financial world into a state of consternation. At the request of the President, Knox announced, the government would soon start a suit under the Sherman Act to dissolve the Northern Securities Company. A good portion of the country cheered the news, but New York and the stock market were temporarily demoralized. Not since the day of McKinley's death, the New York *Tribune* stated, had the market had such "a sudden and severe shock." On the following day Theodore Roosevelt, for the first of many times, became the target of an angry Wall Street. The President's "thunderbolt out of a clear sky" was variously described [by the New York *Tribune* and *Literary Digest*] as "unreasonable" and "beyond comprehension."

The Northern Securities Company was a giant holding company for three large northwestern railroads, the Northern Pacific, the Great Northern, and the Chicago, Burlington and Quincy. The company's architects, J.P. Morgan and Company, the Rockefeller interests, James J. Hill, and E.H. Harriman, were the very Sanhedrin of the nation's railroad and financial oligarchs. This first true holding company had been put together to create a transportation monopoly in the Northwest, and according to the Attorney General it had practically achieved its purpose. Thirty per cent of its capital stock of $400 million was pure water, Knox estimated, a sum representing both an "unwarranted profit" to its organizers and an index to its expected need to overcharge the public.

The magic names of Morgan and [John D.] Rockefeller involved in the Northern Securities suit and the secrecy of its preparation—apparently no one save Roosevelt and Knox had prior news of it—account for the nation's excited reaction to its announcement. A trust-conscious country, fearful of complete domination by further conquests of the New York financial and industrial oligarchy, was cheered by this sudden and energetic use of the long-moribund Sherman Law. When a federal court a year later held the Northern Securities Company illegal and ordered its dissolution, a decision later sustained by the Supreme Court, there was general exultation. No longer was there a question, one journal [*The Outlook*] declared rather optimistically, over whether the giant corporations controlled the people or the people the corporations. "Even Morgan no longer rules the earth," declared another [*Literary Digest*], "and other men may still do business without asking his permission."

The Trust Buster

The promise in the Northern Securities Case for further action under the Sherman Law was not unfulfilled. In the following seven years the Roosevelt administration started similar actions against forty-four corporations, including some of the largest industrial combines in the nation. During the remainder of 1902 only one such suit was originated, that against the so-called beef trust, an action which delighted both the western farmers and the consumers in the city. During 1903 and 1904, an election year, a lull occurred. But in 1905 the antitrust program was once again accelerated, reaching a crescendo in 1906 and 1907, when suits were started against the Standard Oil Company, the American Tobacco Company, the New Haven Railroad, and the Du Pont corporation.

Roosevelt's antitrust activities earned him the name of the "trust buster." At his death in 1919 the Democratic New York *World* suggested that his greatest public service had been rendered when he demonstrated that "the Government of the United States was more powerful than any aggregations of capital. . . ." It is one of history's small ironies that Roosevelt never once in his public life argued that trust busting would cure the industrial problem. As a matter of record, from the time he was governor of New York to the end of his life he believed in government regulation and not dissolution of giant corporations. He stated his position clearly in his first message to Congress, reaffirmed it at Pittsburgh on July 4, 1902, and again all across the country in the campaign of that fall. At Pittsburgh he declared that the growth of large industry was natural, inevitable, and beneficial, and that the nation could no more turn it back by legislation than it could turn back the Mississippi spring floods. But, the President added, we can "regulate and control them by levees."

Why then did Roosevelt launch his attack against monopolies in 1902 and why did he keep at it intermittently during the rest of his administration? There is little direct evidence in the Roosevelt manuscripts to answer the question, but something can be implied.

At a very early age Roosevelt shared the progressives' fear of the rising commercial and industrial oligarchy and its political pretensions. Speaking of labor's misdeeds in 1894, he said that the bankers and railroad men also needed "sound chastisement." In his *Autobiography* he stated bluntly that "of all the forms of tyranny the least attractive and the most vulgar is the tyranny of mere wealth. . . ." Early in Roosevelt's presidency J.P. Morgan came to see him to talk over commercial policy. Roosevelt was beside himself at the tycoon's attitude. Morgan had treated him as he might a rival businessman "who either intended to ruin all of his interests or else could be induced to come to an agreement to ruin none. . . ." Here was a challenge to the President and the nation that Roosevelt had to meet. Roosevelt knew that to attack the trust problem was the one action calculated to win the admiration and support of middle-class America. He was also aware that the conservative-dominated Congress would not pass the required legislation for any effective program of control. Even for his limited 1902 objectives of inspection and publicity he had a "stand-up fight" with [Senator Nelson] Aldrich in early 1903 before he obtained a promise of necessary support. What he had paid for that support is obvious from a memorandum in the manuscripts of Attorney General Knox. The Knox memorandum of February 15, 1903, states that Senator Aldrich had that day brought a note from the President asking Knox to make a public statement on the trust problem, including the statement: "Congress has now enacted all that is practicable and all that is desirable to do." Knox's statement was published the following day, and Congress received no more requests for trust regulation during Roosevelt's first term.

Reelection and Regulation

With the path to effective regulation blocked by a stubborn, conservative Congress, the only way for Roosevelt to bring the arrogant capitalists to heel was through the judicious use of the antitrust laws. The Northern Securities suit, involving Morgan, Rockefeller, and Harriman, was natural for his purpose. During 1903 and 1904 his campaigning against the trusts lagged, but after his re-election he returned to his demands for regulation. In his 1904 annual report, Commissioner of Corporations James R. Garfield, one of the President's bright young men, argued that the only valid way to meet the threat of monopoly was through federal regulation and recommended that all interstate business be licensed by the federal government with a requirement that the licensees be obligated to report annually on the kinds and amounts of business done, together with profits earned. Back in 1903, after he had made his agreement with Aldrich, Roosevelt had called a similar proposal by Senator [George F.] Hoar "idiotic." But in 1906 and again in 1907 he asked Congress to pass such supervisory legislation. Again Congress refused and again the antitrust campaign seemed to be stepped up. There was something almost contrapuntal in Roosevelt's use of the Sherman Law and his demands for federal supervision. Long afterward Roosevelt stated that his antitrust campaign had given the government the power to suppress monopolies and to control holding companies. This was not altogether true, and it is doubtful whether Roosevelt when in office really believed what he was to write in his *Autobiography*. His real views to the contrary were expressed many times. During the campaign of 1908 he argued that the only effective action was to increase greatly "Federal control over all combinations engaged in interstate commerce, instead of relying upon the foolish antitrust law. . . ."

Labor on Strike

Some months after Roosevelt's spectacular action against the Northern Securities Company, the administration was confronted with a labor crisis of major proportions which, had it been handled badly, might have endangered its political future. In May, 1902, over fifty thousand anthracite coal miners enrolled in the United Mine Workers walked off their jobs in northeastern Pennsylvania, demanding a 10 to 20 per cent increase in pay, recognition of the union, an eight-hour day, and other fringe benefits. A similar strike in the preceding election year of 1900 had won a settlement granting a 10 per cent increase, due largely to the mediating influence of Mark Hanna. Hanna had been disturbed by the possible effect of the strike on McKinley's election prospects, and had persuaded the reluctant operators that four more years of McKinley Republicanism was worth a 10 per cent wage raise.

From 70 to 80 per cent of the anthracite fields were owned by six railroads crisscrossing the region. The rail presidents, headed by George F. Baer of the Reading and W.H. Truesdale of the Lackawanna, insisted that this time there should be no political compromise. Relying upon the fuel needs of the seaboard cities from Boston to Washington, they closed down the mines, rejected all offers of negotiation, and waited for the union to crack. Led by the able John F. Mitchell and financed by contributions from the soft-coal miners, the United Mine Workers held their ranks through July, September, and into October. As winter approached even schools and hospitals had empty coalbins, and the public temper became increasingly ugly. Senator [Henry Cabot] Lodge reported that civil commotion was imminent in Boston, and the President felt that there was real danger of riots in New York City. . . .

As early as the middle of June, Roosevelt had sent the Commissioner of Labor into the coal fields to investigate and propose a solution in the event the strike was not soon settled. But despite the almost unanimous approval of the press for government intervention, Roosevelt refused to act during July and August. Since Knox, Roosevelt adviser [Elihu] Root, and Lodge all advised that the government was without constitutional power to intervene, the President found himself at his "wit's end." The whole affair proved to him again that it was necessary to have government supervision over big corporations. As September rounded into October, as temperatures fell and the public pressure mounted, Roosevelt determined to intervene, advice or no advice. On October 1, telegrams went out from the White House inviting the chief coal operators and the union leaders to a conference on October 3. Exactly what took place at the day-long conference has in the past been guessed at. Apparently, [William] Loeb, the presidential secretary, took notes, but the notes have never been unearthed. Among the papers of Philander C. Knox, however, a long unannotated memorandum, hitherto undetected, gives a purported blow-by-blow account of the day's events. According to the Knox memorandum, Roosevelt opened the short morning session at eleven with the disclaimer that he "had any right or duty to intervene in this way on legal grounds." The urgency of the situation and the national interest, however, made his intervention necessary. Mitchell spoke first for the miners. They were prepared to meet the operators at any time to adjust their differences. If such a meeting was not agreeable, the union was willing to accept the findings of an arbitral commission appointed by the President, provided that the operators also agreed to accept its awards. Roosevelt then asked both parties to think over the offer and adjourned the meeting until three o'clock.

Stalemate

At the afternoon session Baer and his colleagues ignored the labor leaders completely and adamantly refused to talk with the unions either directly or indirectly. What the President was asking them to do, miners' representative John B. Markle said, was "to deal with outlaws" who were responsible for the "existing anarchy." Baer then started a long diatribe against the unions, accusing them of daily violence against the fifteen to twenty thousand peaceful miners who wanted to work. If the power of the state of Pennsylvania was not sufficient to meet the challenge to peace, it became the duty of the President to restore order. "Free government," he concluded, was "a contemptible failure if it can only protect the lives and property and secure comfort of the people by compromise with the violaters of law and instigators of violence and crime." After much the same line had been taken by E.B. Thomas, chairman of the board of the Erie Railroad, and by Markle, representing the independent coal operators, David Wilcox, vice-president of the Delaware and Hudson, charged specifically that the miners had committed twenty murders. [UMW president John] Mitchell immediately objected that the charge was false and offered to resign his position if the operators would name the men responsible for the alleged murders and show that they were guilty as charged. Ignoring Mitchell's interruption, the operators demanded that a permanent injunction be granted against the strikers and that the President "put an end to the anarchy in the coal fields" by using the Army, if necessary, as in the Pullman strike, and by starting an immediate suit against the unions under the Sherman Law. When the President finally asked the operators whether they would agree to Mitchell's proposal for arbitration, he was met with a blunt refusal. Upon his further inquiry whether the owners had anything else to suggest, they replied they had no other proposal except that the miners should return to their jobs and leave the determination of their grievances to the decision of the judge of the courts of common pleas in the districts where the mines were located. After twice "insulting" the President and the Attorney General, the operators left the conference without once addressing a word directly to the union representatives. Three days later the Attorney General received a formal petition from the attorney of the Delaware, Lackawanna and Western Railroad, asking that an injunction be issued against the strikers for interference with interstate commerce and that federal troops be sent to Pennsylvania to restore order. The miners, Knox was told on the same day by the vice-president of the Delaware and Hudson Railroad, should be proceeded against as Eugene Debs was proceeded against in Chicago some ten years before.

The President Proposes a Square Deal

During and after the conference Roosevelt was beside himself at the operators' "arrogant stupidity." But the meeting had given him one constructive idea. Suggesting to Root and Knox that they could write letters of protest if they desired to disclaim responsibility, he indicated that he was prepared to send ten thousand federal troops to dispossess the operators and produce coal. By previous constitutional interpretation the President had the authority to send federal troops into a state to assure the exercise of duly authorized federal powers or when they were requested by a governor or a state legislature to preserve peace and order. Nowhere was the right to seize and operate private property even hinted at, much less specified. Nevertheless, the President talked with General J.M. Schofield and through Senator Mathew Quay arranged for the governor of Pennsylvania to request the intervention of federal troops. Spurred by this terrible specter of state socialism, the friends of capital began to move fast. On October 8, Senators Quay and [Boies] Penrose held a conference with John

Mitchell. Two days later, together with Senators Odell and Platt, they met with Baer. On October 11, with Roosevelt's blessing, Root journeyed to New York for a secret conference with J.P. Morgan. The "Great Mogul of Wall Street" was induced to put pressure on the railroad presidents, and at a White House conference on October 13 the groundwork for a compromise was worked out between the President and agents of the acknowledged autocrat of American finance and industry, Morgan. The miners were to go back to work, and a five-man commission appointed by the President, consisting of one Army engineer, a mining engineer, a "businessman familiar with the coal industry," a federal judge, and an "eminent sociologist," was to arbitrate the points at issue. Subsequently the commission was raised to seven members, and the President, in order to meet labor's objections to the one-sided nature of its personnel, agreed to appoint E.E. Clarke, president of the Brotherhood of Railroad Conductors, as the "eminent sociologist." In March, 1903, the commission made public its awards: the miners were given a 10 per cent raise on the average, working hours were reduced in some cases to eight and in most to nine, recognition of the union was not conceded, and the traditional manner of weighing coal was to be continued. The commission also recommended a 10 per cent increase in the price of coal, a proposal of which the operators quickly availed themselves.

During the presidential campaign of 1904 Roosevelt described his actions in the coal strike as simply giving both labor and capital a "square deal." The phrase was to stick in public memory as so many of Roosevelt's did, and perhaps it started the twentieth-century fashion of likening national political programs to phrases in an ethically operated game of chance. The President's actions during the strike set many important precedents. For the first time in a labor dispute representatives of both capital and labor were called to the White House, where the influence of the government was used to obtain a negotiated settlement. For the first time the President had appointed an arbitral board whose decision both sides promised to accept. In order to obtain capital's consent to arbitration, Roosevelt, for the first time in American history, had threatened to use troops to take over and operate a major industry. Whether he would have gone that far or not is problematical. As Root said later, the President was "a bit of a bluffer" at times. But both by his actions and threats Roosevelt had moved the government away from its traditional position of isolation from such economic struggles. The government, by precedent if not by law, had become a third force and partner in major labor disputes.

Trust-Busting Was Driven by Moral Purpose

Leroy G. Dorsey

Theodore Roosevelt was driven by strong moral convictions and a sense of public duty and service. These factors can be used to understand his crusading efforts to regulate corporations and "bust" trusts. Although the president considered trusts to be natural by-products of a competitive economy, some of them had shown to lack a sense of responsibility to their employees or the community. When this was the case, or when trusts had grown too powerful, Roosevelt intervened. Leroy G. Dorsey is a professor of speech communication at Texas A&M University.

P UBLIC CONCERN OVER THE EMERGENCE OF THE INDUSTRI-al combines at the turn of the twentieth century has been well documented. The frequency at which these trusts were created startled many people. According to some accounts, the public grew more and more apprehensive with the centralized economic power of corporations and their seeming ability to swallow or to ruin effective competitors and to control consumer prices at will. The middle class' initial surprise at these new business entities quickly turned to fear. For those people, the growth of large manufacturing corporations and holding companies

Excerpted from "Theodore Roosevelt and Corporate America, 1901–1909: A Reexamination," by Leroy G. Dorsey, *Presidential Studies Quarterly*, Fall 1995. Copyright © 1995 by Sage Publications, Inc. Reproduced by permission.

appeared ready to stifle their own economic opportunities. And with continued publicity being given to many corporations' questionable business practices, public fears soon turned to hatred. No sooner would some business be labeled a trust than it would be denounced as a conspiracy. The majority of the American people, [historian] David Noble has concluded, was not convinced that "their future lay within a corporate society."

All this was not lost on Theodore Roosevelt. In reflecting back upon his presidency in his autobiography, he recalled that the attitude of the nation toward corporate businesses represented one of the most vital questions he faced. While President, Roosevelt struggled not only to counter the growing public animosity regarding these new business entities, but to curb their excesses that helped give rise to the public's animosity. Roosevelt viewed the anti-business fervor fueled by journalistic "muck-rakers" as just as dangerous as the excessive greed of corporate officers. Thus, Stephen Lucas has concluded that the President sought a middle ground in the hopes to "minimize dangers from extremists on both ends."

With social order as his overriding concern, President Roosevelt used the "bully pulpit" to urge restraint by both big business and its muckraking critics and to lessen the attendant apprehension of the American people. . . .

Roosevelt's Record

Roosevelt's record concerning the supervision of corporate activity has been a point of contention for decades. Some historians have given him credit for several noteworthy accomplishments. For example, William Letwin has applauded the President's "brilliant defeat" of the railroad holding company, Northern Securities, by invoking the little used Sherman Antitrust Act. Arthur Johnson has noted that the President worked successfully to create a Bureau of Corporations that would publicly report on corporate abuses. George Mowry has acknowledged Roosevelt's direct responsibility for the passage of the Hepburn Act. For Mowry, this legislation represented a "landmark in the evolution of federal control of private industry."

For some, however, Roosevelt's tough, "Rough Riding" cowboy image did not extend to his relationship with big business. According to biographer Henry Pringle, Roosevelt's image as a "trust buster" was an exaggeration. In almost apologetic tones, Pringle has noted that Roosevelt initiated only twenty-five suits under the Sherman Antitrust Act, while his successor, William Taft, started forty-five. Gabriel Kolko likewise has questioned Roosevelt's use of the Sherman Antitrust Act. Kolko has charged that the Northern Securities case was politically popular but that it failed to alter the railroad situation in the Northwest. Lewis Gould has noted the ineffectiveness of the Bureau of Corporations when dealing with the beef trust, calling it a public-relations nightmare that embarrassed the Administration. Gould has also observed that the Hepburn Act probably did more harm than good to the nation's transportation system. Johnson has concluded that Roosevelt's inconsistent means to distinguish between "good" and "bad" trusts on a moral basis proved impossible to institutionalize into sound legislative policy.

Several scholars have also generally dismissed the President's rhetoric concerning the trusts. Gould, for example, has concluded that despite the rhetorical furor over antitrust cases early in his presidency, there was no dramatic increase in antitrust cases in Roosevelt's first term. Grant McConnell has pronounced that Roosevelt's actions were less impressive than the "noise" accompanying them. Finally, Richard Hofstadter has argued that there was a "hundred times more noise than accomplishment" in the President's antitrust suits and that the "most intense and rapid growth of trusts in American business history" occurred on Roosevelt's watch.

The view that Roosevelt made less than substantive gains in the antitrust area often rests upon the distinction between his deeds and his rhetoric. Viewed from the latter perspective, however, Roosevelt actually accomplished a great deal. He did not break up many trusts, but he did provide a sympathetic ear and a powerful voice for the unfocused discontent of the country regarding the growth and abusive practices of corporations and trusts. With his public rhetoric, the President led a symbolic crusade against impersonal and amoral forces. He took growing public resentment of big business, moderated its radicalism, and refocused it to create the pressure needed to persuade Congress to pass reform legislation such as the Hepburn Act. In other words, he provided Americans with an outlet for their frustration. In his continuous scouring of the "criminal rich," biographer William Harbaugh has noted, Roosevelt gave his audiences the satisfaction of "emotional catharsis."

Perhaps most importantly, Roosevelt's rhetoric put pressure upon big business to reform itself. At a time when many business leaders viewed the federal government as a "second rate" power, Roosevelt seized the legislative and moral high ground to try and restrain wholesale corporate abuses. He believed that the very threat of anti-trust legislation might convince corporate leaders to do business in the proper spirit of public service. He put the captains of industry on notice that if they failed to police themselves, to engage in what he considered moral behavior, then government would be forced to intervene.

As some scholars have conceded, Roosevelt's "strong language had value in itself." Hofstadter has contended that despite the ambiguity in Roosevelt's rhetoric, an ambiguity that is the heart of practical politics, his rhetoric transcended the "weak and halting" equivocations of most ordinary politicians and displayed a "fine aggressive surge." Similarly, Pringle offers the conclusion that there was "significance" in what Roosevelt "said rather than what he did."

In all these senses, Roosevelt accomplished quite a lot. As Harbaugh has concluded:

> at a time when the American people's government was perilously close to becoming a mere satellite of big business, Theodore Roosevelt, by a masterful assertion of both his moral and political authority, had reaffirmed the people's right to control their affairs through their elected representatives.

Particularly during his first term, President Roosevelt sought to educate the nation about big business, hoping to ease the public's anxiety regarding corporations and trusts, and to temper those journalists stoking the nation's unease. Breaking with presidential tradition and speaking

What Would TR Do?

Leading Theodore Roosevelt scholar Edmund Morris ponders what his subject would do about corporations if he were president today.

It's tempting to speculate how TR might behave as president if he were alive today. The honest answer, of course, is that he would be bewildered by the strangeness of everything, as people blind from birth are said to be when shocked by the "gift" of sight. But he certainly would be appalled by contemporary Americans' vulgarity and sentimentality, particularly the way we celebrate nonentities. Also by our lack of respect for officeholders and teachers, lack of concern for unborn children, excessive wealth and deteriorating standards of physical fitness.

Abroad he would admire our willingness to challenge foreign despots and praise the generosity with which we finance the development of less-fortunate economies. At

about such non-constitutional issues, Roosevelt frequently addressed the public about its attitudes and beliefs. Furthermore, as a rhetorical president, he understood the need to address simultaneously the varied interest groups of the nation. To that end, he engaged a line of argument that was at once educational and compelling. Roosevelt's rhetoric was compelling, in part, because it was primarily metaphoric in nature. . . .

The Moral Standard

Strategically, Roosevelt concentrated on the railroad industry for two reasons. Not only did existing laws fail to stop monopolistic combinations in this industry, but according to some accounts, railroad combines actually favored the most ruthless industrial corporations. More im-

---

home he would want to do something about Microsoft, since he had been passionate about monopoly from the moment he entered politics. Although no single trust a hundred years ago approached the monolithic immensity of Mr. [Bill] Gates' empire, the Northern Securities merger of 1901 created the greatest transport combine in the world, controlling commerce from Chicago to China.

TR busted it. In doing so he burnished himself with instant glory as the champion of American individual enterprise against corporate "malefactors of great wealth." That reputation suited him just fine, although he privately believed in Big Business and was just as wary of unrestrained, amateurish competition. All he wanted to establish, early in his first term, was government's right to regulate rampant entrepreneurship.

Edmund Morris, "Theodore Roosevelt: With Limitless Energy and a Passionate Sense of the Nation, He Set the Stage for the American Century," *Time*, vol. 151, no. 14, April 13, 1998, pp. 78–80.

portantly, perhaps, he understood the importance of the railroad industry to the material prosperity of the nation. Thus, he sought to persuade railroad owners to rehabilitate themselves before public backlash promoted the need for extreme corrective measures against all corporate entities.

Beyond working to educate the public about the natural evolution of corporate businesses, Roosevelt also took up the rhetorical task of ensuring that these businesses would exhibit the proper civic responsibility. His crusade against big business' amoral behavior began with what he and many others considered the most powerful and corrupt trust: the railroad combines. At the turn of the twentieth century, many people feared that the railroad corporations sought to place the "entire American transportation system under an oligarchy of three or four powerful men." Such was the reputation of J.P. Morgan, James Hill, and Edward Harriman that when they formed their railroad corporation in 1901, Northern Securities, the "question was raised as to whether such a combination might eventually control the entire United States." This railroad trust engaged in several questionable practices. For example, by monopolizing transportation in the Northwest, small shippers faced no other recourse but to pay the charges fixed by the trust. In addition, the union of these railroads caused their stock to be valued at a degree substantially higher than its worth, bringing their owners an unwarranted profit.

Not only did railroad trusts sometimes overcharge the public but they also gave special rates to particular corporate clients. According to Roosevelt, corporations such as Standard Oil received "secret rates" from the railroad companies which aided it in maintaining a virtual monopoly in its field. Essentially, by assuring the railroad company of substantial business, Standard Oil received a rate lower than other, smaller shippers. With lower transportation expenses, Roosevelt contended in a 1906 Message to Congress, Standard Oil unfairly operated at a more profitable level than its competitors: "the profit of course comes not merely by the saving in the rate itself as compared with its competitors, but by the higher prices [Standard Oil] is able to charge . . . by the complete control of the market which it secures. . . ." This, Roosevelt claimed, represented a "characteristic example" of the "numerous evils" which had been occurring under a "system in which the big shipper and the railroad are left free to crush out all individual initiative."

Thus, upon entering the White House, Roosevelt threw down the gauntlet. The White House announced that it would initiate a suit under the Sherman Antitrust Act to dissolve the Northern Securities Company. The Sherman Antitrust Act had passed eleven years earlier, but until 1902, had rarely been invoked by a Chief Executive: Presidents Harrison, Cleveland, and McKinley had initiated a total of only eighteen suits under that law. By going after Northern Securities, an entity that in Roosevelt's view personified big business, with a law so rarely invoked, the President assured a trust-conscious nation that those industrial oligarchies engaged in suspect business practices would not go unchallenged.

As a rhetorical president, Roosevelt used the attack on Northern Securities as a "media event" to promote the need for rate regulation of the railroad industry. On this issue, he met with determined resistance. Several corporate leaders denounced rate regulation, including railroad owners and coal operators. Not only were these groups well organized, but they "overwhelmed congressmen with petitions and telegrams." The railroad trusts even engaged in a publicity campaign in 1905 to sway public opinion in their favor concerning rate regulation. Because of these private efforts, coupled with a resistant Congress, Roosevelt took his case to the public. He traveled across the nation not only to generate support for rate regulation, but perhaps more importantly, to bring a stronger sense of public service to corporate leaders.

Just as Roosevelt defended the corporate form of business by employing Darwinian imagery, he utilized Darwinian metaphors in his attack. Careful not to excite unnecessarily the nation, Roosevelt reminded it that *all* corporations were part of the natural order; however, *some* corporations threatened that order. As wild animals in the jungle preyed upon one another, certain trusts also could be labeled as predatory. While some such behavior might be natural in a competitive business environment, Roosevelt drew the line at success brought about by "vulpine cunning" and "wolfish greed." Too many businessmen, he told a Georgia audience in 1905, used the "noxious phrase" of "business is business" as a justification for every type of "mean and crooked work." Too often, Roosevelt declared before a crowd assembled for the dedication of a monument, did the "predatory capitalist" win his fortune "by chicanery and wrong-doing" that hurt the public good. According to the President, railroad owners deliberately manipulated railroad stock rather than manage their businesses efficiently and honestly. In several public addresses, Roosevelt charged that the rapacious owners of the railroad trusts engaged in "insolent and manifold abuses" including bribery, neglect of employee safety, and deliberate evasion of laws. In what [scholar William] Harbaugh has called Roosevelt's "most bitter and radical" Special Message, the President condemned such behavior as not only criminal but immoral. In that 1908 Message, he likened metaphorically some corporate leaders to predatory parasites:

> Just as the black-mailer and the bribe giver stand on the same evil eminence of infamy, so the man who makes an enormous fortune by corrupting legislatures and municipalities and fleecing his stockholder and the public, stands on the same moral level with the creature who fattens on the blood money of the gambling-house and the saloon.

By casting the railroad trust as a wild predator, Roosevelt

captured public support for legislation to curb its abuses. . . .

Roosevelt believed that he had to stop the rampant excesses of some of the rich corporate owners who embodied an enervating, materialistic spirit. Otherwise, they threatened not only their own spiritual health but also the material and spiritual well-being of the entire nation. The President believed that civilizations collapsed when their people concentrated solely on material wealth. He maintained that the worship of luxury, and the immoral manner in which the corporate owners were acquiring it, weakened the more traditional, spiritual virtues of thrift, hard work, and a basic sense of right. When that occurred, civilizations declined. "If ever our people become so sordid," Roosevelt declared before a 1907 Mississippi audience, "as to feel that all that counts is moneyed prosperity, ignoble well-being, [and] effortless ease and comfort, then this nation shall perish."

Using his bully pulpit, Roosevelt preached not only to the railroad oligarchs, but to all the corporate leaders that their immoral behavior harmed the nation. Some men of "swollen fortune," he warned the National Educational Association in 1905, served as a "bad example." Their success by immoral means set up a "false standard" for the country to follow. Furthermore, the "exaggerated importance" corporate leaders gave to wealth aroused the envy of others and generally promoted "sour and discontented" feelings. "Venomous envy of wealth . . . [and] cringing servility toward wealth," Roosevelt asserted, "springs from a fantastically twisted . . . idea of the importance of wealth as compared to other things." This, he warned a Georgia audience in 1905, was the "worst damage" that corporate leaders could do to the country:

> the awakening in our breasts of either the mean vice of
> worshipping mere wealth, and the man of mere wealth,
> for the wealth's sake, or the equally mean vice of view-

ing with rancorous envy and hatred the men of wealth merely because they are men of wealth.

Similar to that of a minister delivering a sermon to his congregation, Roosevelt's public messages called for the moral rehabilitation of the owners behind the trusts. He hoped to awaken the corporate leaders to the fact that their immorality harmed not only the nation, but themselves as well. In no uncertain terms, Roosevelt told the corporate owner who raced after material wealth that such a life produced only evil: an evil realized by a "carelessness toward the rights of others." This mean-spirited arrogance, he warned, led business leaders to disregard their obligations to the country and to neglect the "rights and the needs of those who are less well off." In Roosevelt's eyes what made the misdeeds of these "malefactors of great wealth" so repugnant was the fact that they committed their transgressions with "no excuse of want, of poverty, of weakness and ignorance to offer as partial atonement." In short, they lacked basic moral decency. It was time, Roosevelt declared in his December 1905 Annual Message, that the corporate leaders followed a moral standard for business:

> There can be no delusion more fatal to the nation, than the delusion that the standard of profits . . . is sufficient in judging any business [question]. Business success . . . is a good thing only so far as it is accompanied by and develops a high standard of conduct—honor, integrity, civic courage.

In a sense, then, Roosevelt's "anti-trust" rhetoric might be more appropriately termed as "pro-business" rhetoric. Not only did he attempt to protect the good name of honest businesses but also to safeguard them from hostile public sentiment. Roosevelt feared that the unrestrained lawlessness of trusts such as the railroad combines to acquire wealth would only come back to haunt them. Material well-being thus had to be placed within the proper perspective: as a foundation upon which the moral concerns of a people would be preeminent. If corporate leaders and the public failed to embrace this proper attitude toward big business, Roosevelt suggested, America was doomed to the fate of other failed civilizations.

Roosevelt's Moral Crusade

Theodore Roosevelt faced a particularly vexing problem during his presidency. On the one hand, corporations represented powerful and profitable business entities that he believed could enhance the material prosperity of the nation. On the other hand, these same corporations sometimes engaged in illegal, and in his mind, immoral practices. Furthermore, he believed that the public's cries of dissatisfaction and anger regarding these illegalities threatened the social order. As a rhetorical president, Roosevelt took his case to the public. He hoped to reconcile both the business and anti-business interests as well as to preserve the order and stability necessary for America to realize its destiny as a materially and spiritually-rich nation.

According to Roosevelt, big business provided a material foundation for America's spiritual growth. To that end, he defended it against what he considered unwarranted public hostility and muck-raking journalism. Using metaphors to educate and to argue for big business, Roosevelt portrayed the industrial combines as necessary parts for the health of the American body. In Darwinian terms, the trusts became natural results of economic evolution. Finally, to calm public animosity, Roosevelt condemned those journalists who wrote lurid and exaggerated accounts of corporate abuses, portraying them as unqualified doctors prescribing questionable remedies for corporate wrongdoings. From his bully pulpit, the President hoped to restrain the agitative rhetoric of the muck-rakers and to change the public's image of the trusts.

Roosevelt also went after those trusts that he felt deserved criticism, most notably the railroad combines. Likening the railroad corporations metaphorically to predators, Roosevelt pushed for federal rate regulation. Yet government legislation, in his view, resembled a dealer in a card game: it could ensure everyone had a "square deal," but it could not ensure that all participants would play fairly. What was not needed, the President believed, was intrusive and stifling regulations. What he called for was a spirit of moral responsibility among the captains of industry.

Thus, Roosevelt's efforts involving the trusts may be seen as primarily a moral crusade. Critics who measure Roosevelt's success by the number of anti-trust suits he brought or won miss the essentially rhetorical purposes of his crusade. Scholars who characterize him as "all talk" and who condemn him for not accomplishing enough fail to understand exactly what the President hoped to achieve. Roosevelt viewed the trusts as vital to America's well-being and he never sought to dismantle them or to render them impotent. The legislative "stick" only threatened to fall in the absence of moral principle. For Roosevelt, big business could be properly regulated only by individual morality and a spirit of public service.

Essentially, the problem of the trusts involved a matter of character. Some corporations, and some individuals, suffered from flaws in their character. As with most causes in Roosevelt's career, the controversy over corporate America could be reduced to the values that its leaders embraced. He exploited the powers of the rhetorical presidency to preach lessons about corporate leaders' social responsibility and their moral principles. In doing so, he legitimated the spirit of progressive reform regarding corporate business. Far from being a failed trust buster, Theodore Roosevelt revolutionized the American business community by instilling in it a standard of moral and social accountability.

CHAPTER

3

EXPANDING AMERICA'S ROLE IN THE WORLD

Roosevelt Is the Father of American Internationalism

Fareed Zakaria

Most books credit President Woodrow Wilson, who served from 1913 to 1921, with American internationalism. After all, Wilson was president during World War I, and it was he who proposed the idea of the League of Nations. However, Fareed Zakaria believes that it was Theodore Roosevelt who deserves credit as the first to promote a prominent role for the United States in the international order. Zakaria, an author and international relations scholar, further argues that Wilson's views were unrealistic, whereas Roosevelt, with a peace-through-strength philosophy and an engaged foreign policy, offered a more pragmatic notion of internationalism.

FOR ALMOST 50 YEARS AMERICANS HAVE ASSOCIATED A RObust internationalism with a particular outlook on the world, Wilsonianism. As we see the latter floundering in the post–Cold War world, many have concluded that the former is also in trouble. But the two are unconnected; Wilsonianism is dying, internationalism is not. In fact, as the United States recognizes the limits of Wilsonianism it will be able to return to an older tradition of American statecraft and construct a sober and purposeful relation-

Excerpted from "Internationalism as a Way of Life," by Fareed Zakaria, *World Policy Journal*, Summer 1995. Copyright © 1995 by *World Policy Journal*. Reprinted with permission.

ship to the new and complicated world it is in, one that promotes American interests and ideals in a realistic way. The model for a new American internationalism is not Woodrow Wilson, but his great rival, Theodore Roosevelt.

Wilson's World

Woodrow Wilson believed that America should transform international politics rather than engage in it. The goal of American foreign policy, he explained in his request of Congress for a declaration of war in 1917, was the creation of "a universal dominion of right by such a concert of free peoples as shall bring peace and safety to all nations and make the world free at last." Such a world would be governed by laws and arbitration. The defense of any country would be ensured by a rule-based collective security system, where every member state pledges to come to the defense of any other member state. Naturally, this meant that any opponent of American foreign policy was an obstacle on the path to justice, and a moral crusade against such a transgressor was the only proper course. As Wilson said, "Right is more precious than peace."

Because Wilson saw the world in moral, rather than strategic, terms, he believed America had interests in every corner of the globe. He even saw Washington's Farewell Address, long regarded as the cardinal text of isolationism, as sanctioning his globalism. [Former secretary of state and historian] Henry Kissinger remarks on this sophistry:

> Proving that the time spent in faculty meetings had not been wasted, where hairsplitting exegesis reigns supreme, [Wilson] developed an extraordinary interpretation of what George Washington meant when he warned against foreign entanglements. Wilson redefined "foreign" in a way that would surely have astonished the first president. What Washington meant, according to Wilson, was that America must avoid becoming entangled in the purposes of others. But, Wilson argued, nothing that concerns

humanity "can be foreign or indifferent to us." Hence America had an unlimited charter to involve itself abroad.

Balance of Power Politics

Wilsonianism is an inspiring but impractical way of looking at the world. When Wilson tried to sell his grand scheme, the League of Nations, to his own countrymen in 1919, they balked. The Senate rightly believed that membership in the League would mean that the United States could be drawn into war without the sanction of Congress. When the League was tried in Europe after the First World War, it failed. What later rescued Europe from tyranny was not Wilson's rule-based collective security system, but rather old-fashioned balance-of-power politics. When— and only when—Germany posed a threat to the region as a whole, a balancing alliance of great powers formed against it. By the 1930s the only Wilsonians were World Federalists. Had it not been for the Cold War, the legacy of Wilsonianism might have had only an inspirational, rather than an operational, effect on American foreign policy.

The Cold War turned foreign policy into a great moral struggle that could end only in an uncompromising victory for one side. The world was confronted by two diametrically opposed philosophies of government, spearheaded by two great and ambitious powers. The struggle was played out on a global scale, partly because of the universalist nature of the conflict, partly because of the bipolar nature of the world, in which the two superpowers—and particularly the United States—towered over every region of the globe. American foreign policy was properly aimed at the transformation of the Soviet Union, because the Soviet Union was not a normal great power playing by normal rules. This peculiar situation meant Wilsonianism fit nicely into the rhetoric and reality of America's Cold War policy.

But the Cold War is over. Of the two defining features

of that post-1945 world, the great ideological and strategic Soviet threat is gone and America's unrivaled economic

---

I Believe

In his autobiography, Theodore Roosevelt reflects on his leadership in international affairs.

In internal affairs I cannot say that I entered the Presidency with any deliberately planned and far-reaching scheme of social betterment. I had, however certain strong convictions; and I was on the lookout for every opportunity of realizing those convictions. I was bent upon making the Government the most efficient possible instrument in helping the people of the United States to better themselves in every way, politically, socially, and industrially. I believed with all my heart in real and thoroughgoing democracy, and I wished to make this democracy industrial as well as political, although I had only partially formulated the methods I believed we should follow. I believed in the people's rights, and therefore in National rights and States' rights just exactly to the degree in which they severally secured popular rights. I believed in invoking the National power with absolute freedom for every National need; and I believed that the Constitution should be treated as the greatest document ever devised by the wit of man to aid a people in exercising every power necessary for its own betterment, and not as a straitjacket cunningly fashioned to strangle growth. As for the particular methods of realizing these various beliefs, I was content to wait and see what method might be necessary in each given case as it arose; and I was certain that the cases would arise fast enough.

Theodore Roosevelt, *Theodore Roosevelt: An Autobiography.* New York: Scribner's, 1913, pp. 385–86.

position is diminished. None of the great powers pose a moral or material threat to the United States in the way that the Soviet Union did. Most of them are trying to become modern industrial states. The crucial strategic power centers of the world, western Europe and East Asia, are currently characterized by great-power peace and prosperity. For its part, the United States is still the strongest nation in the world, but it cannot act on all its moral preferences everywhere. The costs are too high, the benefits are too few. The Clinton administration's initial attempts to conduct foreign policy along Wilsonian lines, and the failure of that effort from Bosnia to China, have caused the halting realization that America cannot implement a Wilsonian foreign policy.

TR's Vision

The world in which Theodore Roosevelt came to power in 1901 has many things in common with the world today. It was characterized by peace among the great powers and an ever-widening zone of liberty. Capitalism and free trade were on the rise, and regimes everywhere were liberalizing. Even some of the specifics were the same: a rising Japan in the East, a newly unified Germany in Europe, and a Russia obsessed by its internal troubles. Economically, America, then as now, was the greatest of the great powers, having 20–25 percent of world GNP (roughly its share today). But it had not converted its economic power into military and diplomatic strength. This became Roosevelt's great challenge. He saw the introduction of the United States onto the world stage, not simply as an act of national egotism, but as necessary for the proper functioning of the international system. He believed that America, like Britain, had to play a role as an offshore balancer, ensuring that vital areas of the world—Europe and East Asia—did not fall prey to one dominant power. This explains his position in the Russo-Japanese War of 1904, in which he wanted neither side to enjoy a decisive victory. "It is best that [Russia] should be left to face Japan so that each may have a moderative influence on the other."

Roosevelt believed, above all else, in national power. He dismissed the possibility of "establishing any kind of international power . . . which can effectively check wrongdoing" and regarded as "abhorrent" the "Wilson-Bryan attitude of trusting to fantastic peace treaties, to impossible promises, to all kinds of scraps of paper without any backing in efficient force." He distrusted legalism, knowing that nation-states interpreted their own interests as they saw fit. International laws or organizations could not stop them from doing this, but countervailing force could moderate their behavior. Thus, he was an advocate of a strong military, or of "preparedness," as it was then called. He believed that the maintenance of ready power was not just a useful tool, but a great deterrent. "The most important service that I rendered to peace," he once explained, "was the voyage of the battle fleet round the world."

I Believe

He has often been charged, somewhat contradictorily, of being a pure realist and a passionate imperialist. Neither is quite true. Roosevelt believed that nations inevitably had spheres of interest; unstable areas close to them that would impinge on their own security. When he intervened in Central America, in Santo Domingo in 1905, and in Cuba, reluctantly, in 1906, he did so not because he had dreams of ruling a great Central American empire, but rather because he wanted to preclude the possibility that the European great powers would, either out of nervousness or ambition, regard the local instability as a cause to intervene themselves. He cordoned off that part of the world from European great-power rivalry. He withdrew as often as he intervened, pulling out of Cuba once the local government was able to maintain order. Like the naval theorist Alfred

Thayer Mahan, he wanted to annex certain strategic positions, such as the Panama Canal, but he did not want territory for territory's sake. In 1912, he gave up the Philippines because he decided that the costs of their defense far outweighed the strategic benefits.

For the Good of Humanity

Nor was he a rank realist. It has become commonplace to judge American statesmen against the messianic program of Woodrow Wilson and, finding them lacking in moral fervor, to brand them amoral. Roosevelt believed that America was a special country and that its foreign policy should help promote its principles. He understood that not all regimes were the same; he regarded German power as threatening but British power as benign. He did not, however, believe that the spread of his principles was a crusade to be undertaken by the United States alone, or that this could be accomplished by a conspicuously moralistic foreign policy that almost by definition asked America to spurn its own interests for the good of humanity.

In a sense, Roosevelt had greater confidence in American ideals than Wilson did. Roosevelt believed that the progress of "civilization" was ongoing. And it was the task of all the civilized great powers, though in particular of Britain and the United States. The greatest service the United States could do to promote liberty in the world was to ensure great-power peace and the resulting spread of global prosperity.

Roosevelt Empowered the Presidency and Expanded U.S. Influence

Walter Lafeber

After the Spanish-American War in 1898, the United States found itself a global military power with a reach into Latin America and the Pacific. Similarly, the nation had emerged as a global economic power. Questions existed, however, as to whether America's efforts to extend its sphere of influence were constitutional. In the following essay, Walter Lafeber writes that by expanding the definition of the common defense clause of the Constitution, Roosevelt empowered the presidency to expand American interests worldwide. Walter Lafeber is a distinguished professor of history at Cornell University and author of *America, Russia, and the Cold War* and *Inevitable Revolutions: The United States in Central America.*

I N 1900 THE UNITED STATES WAS EMERGING FOR THE FIRST time as a great world power. As a result of the 1898 war against Spain, the American military reach stretched from Latin America to China. After a half-century of incredible industrialization, the U.S. economic reach stretched around the globe. European observers warned that dollars served as the cutting edge for an American invasion of Old World markets. Many of those dollars were held by the first Unit-

Excerpted from "'The Lion in the Path': The U.S. Emergence as a World Power," by Walter Lafeber, *Political Science Quarterly*, 1986. Copyright © 1986 by The Academy of Political Science. Reprinted with permission.

ed States multinational corporations, which had appeared in the 1880s and 1890s. In Asia, U.S. officials issued two historic "open door" notes, which asked the other powers to observe Chinese territorial integrity and, as Secretary of State John Hay phrased it, "a fair field and no favor" in the intensifying competition for China's vast markets. To protect these multiplying interests, the United States Navy, which had ranked below the top dozen fleets (including Chile's) just a decade earlier, suddenly grew into one of the five largest navies by 1900. It could use newly seized bases, moreover, that included the Philippines, Guam, Hawaii, Cuba, and Puerto Rico. In a moment of conquest during the late 1890s, the nation had transformed itself from a continental to a global power. The American Century had begun.

The fundamental question for the U.S. political system was whether the Constitution of 1787 could provide an adequate plan of government for the new global giant. What the Founders termed "the common defense" in the late eighteenth century in no way resembled the defense needs of early twentieth-century America. Indeed, the term "for the common defense" had apparently been inserted into the Constitution with little thought and less debate. It had appeared in the Articles of Confederation (which the delegates gathered at Philadelphia in the summer of 1787 were about to overthrow), and the Constitutional Convention inserted the words as part of a brief catchall description of the purposes for which a new Congress could levy taxes. James Madison much later recalled that the Philadelphia Convention, the state conventions which ratified the Constitution, and the First Congress under the Constitution accepted "the common defense and general welfare" provision with little concern, although he admitted he quickly became worried after Alexander Hamilton demonstrated how the phrase could be used to justify the exercise of national, and especially presidential, powers that Madison deemed unconstitutional during the 1790s. . . .

Expanding the "Common Defense"

Using the newly acquired Philippine base as a point of embarkation, [President William] McKinley ordered 5,000 troops into the mainland of China in 1900. He ostensibly sent them to protect U.S. lives and property, but the President also wanted the army to help other powers control the Boxer Rebellion and—of particular urgency—watch those powers' colonial ambitions closely. The Japanese and the Europeans had already violated the open-door policy by seizing and closing off parts of the Chinese Empire. McKinley and his successor, Theodore Roosevelt, feared that the Russians intended to colonize vast areas of Manchuria. The Chinese actually declared war on the United States because of this military intervention, but the episode is more important because it set a historic precedent that the president, without express authorization from Congress, could intervene in a sovereign nation and, without that nation's consent, go about reordering its political affairs—including the putting down of revolutionary activity. Until McKinley's action, presidents who had ordered such landings had vowed they were only protecting U.S. lives and property while acting neutrally in the other country's affairs. Following McKinley's lead, Theodore Roosevelt and Woodrow Wilson repeatedly dispatched troops over the next twenty years to Haiti, Santo Domingo [now the Dominican Republic], Nicaragua, Panama, Cuba, Mexico, and finally Russia to play a role in deciding the outcome of civil wars.

Maintaining the common defense of the United States was beginning to mean repeated military intervention in the internal affairs of other nations, some as close as Mexico, others as distant as China and the Soviet Union. But by 1900, distance was less important in foreign relations than it had been earlier. Certainly it was less significant than in 1787. The transportation and communications revolutions had produced what [Constitutional law expert] Louis Fisher calls the "shrinking globe" theory of U.S. foreign policy. Throughout much of the nineteenth century Washington officials had fashioned a defensive war rationale to justify the use of power to defend, or more usually to extend, their country's borders. In 1898, however, McKinley partly justified intervention in Cuba by claiming the problem was "right at our door." Fisher rightly argues that the "shrinking world" view took hold only after World War II, but a half-century earlier McKinley's, Roosevelt's, and Wilson's interventions in neighboring countries provided strong evidence for Fisher's observation that the "idea of a shrinking globe has been part of the conceptual shift behind the enlargement of presidential power." As he neatly summarized the effect of the principle, "constitutionally it shrinks not merely the globe but congressional power as well."

The Founders had carefully delegated the war-declaring powers to Congress and the war-making powers to the executive, but by 1900 both powers were largely in the president's hands. The Senate occasionally tried to arouse itself and reclaim its earlier authority. In 1901 it rejected an Anglo-American treaty that gave the United States the right to build but not defend an isthmian canal. The Senate demanded the authority to defend a new passageway as well. The defeat of the agreement led the self-pitying Secretary of State, John Hay, to compare a treaty entering the Senate to a bull entering the bullring. Not the result but only the moment of death was unpredictable, Hay lamented. Historians have paid more attention to Hay's remarks than have presidents. Theodore Roosevelt admired Hay, but the new President disliked Hay's treaty. The secretary of state consequently negotiated a second, more advantageous pact that gave the United States all it wanted. The agreement quickly gained Senate ratification.

Redefining the Monroe Doctrine

In 1904–1905 Roosevelt raised to historic levels both the power of the president to conduct foreign policy without the consent of Congress and the authority to expand the boundaries of the common defense. In this case the defense of U.S. interests involved a radical redefinition of the Monroe Doctrine. In his 1823 declaration, President James Monroe had issued certain principles that were to have long lives: the United States refused to recognize further colonization of the New World by non-western-hemisphere nations; it wanted European powers to keep hands off the Latin American revolutions; and the United States, for its part, declared it did not want to become involved in European affairs unrelated to its own interests. For most of the nineteenth century, the limits of their military power forced Washington officials to restrict the application of the Monroe Doctrine principles to the North American continent. In 1870, however, President Ulysses S. Grant attempted to annex Santo Domingo, a site that held an especially magnificent port coveted by Grant and some of his close, highly corrupt friends in the private sector. The Senate rejected Grant's scheme, but the President nevertheless took the occasion to add a fourth principle to the Monroe Doctrine: henceforth no territory in the New World could be regarded as subject to transfer to a European power. In 1904, Santo Domingo again came into view of U.S. officials. Internal instability, complicated by claims made by French and German companies on the country's resources, threatened both the nation's independence and U.S. shipping and financial interests. Theodore Roosevelt dispatched the U.S. Navy to restore order, took over the customs houses to ensure that the Europeans would be properly paid off and have no excuse to land troops of their own, then justified his action by arguing that as the hemisphere's greatest power the United States had the responsibility to act as a "policeman" who maintained order among unruly, less-developed peoples.

Monroe Doctrine

Several parts of Roosevelt's policy proved to be of special importance. The first appeared when he asked the Senate to ratify a treaty, made between U.S. officials and the Santo

---

Monroe Doctrine

In his own words, Roosevelt describes his view of the Monroe Doctrine.

The Monroe Doctrine lays down the rule that the Western Hemisphere is not hereafter to be treated as subject to settlement and occupation by Old World powers. It is not international law; but it is a cardinal principle of our foreign policy. There is no difficulty at the present day in maintaining this doctrine, save where the American power whose interest is threatened has shown itself in international matters both weak and delinquent. The great and prosperous civilized commonwealths, such as the Argentine, Brazil, and Chile, in the southern half of South America, have advanced so far that they no longer stand in any position of tutelage toward the United States. They occupy toward us precisely the position that Canada occupies. Their friendship is the friendship of equals for equals. My view was that as regards these nations there was no more necessity for asserting the Monroe Doctrine than there was to assert it in regard to Canada. They were competent to assert it for themselves. Of course if one of these nations, or if Canada, should be overcome by some Old World power, which then proceeded to occupy its territory, we would undoubtedly, if the American Nation needed our help, give it in order to prevent such occupation from taking place. But the initiative would come from the Nation itself, and the United States would merely

Domingo government, that allowed Roosevelt's appointees to operate the small nation's customs houses. The Senate refused to ratify, largely on the ground that it did not think the United States should assume a protectorate over the Caribbean country. Several of the more cynical legislators went farther and questioned whether U.S. military power should be deployed for the purpose of firming up the price

act as a friend whose help was invoked.

The case was (and is) widely different as regards certain—not all—of the tropical states in the neighborhood of the Caribbean Sea. Where these states are stable and prosperous, they stand on a footing of absolute equality with all other communities. But some of them have been a prey to such continuous revolutionary misrule as to have grown impotent either to do their duties to outsiders or to enforce their rights against outsiders. The United States has not the slightest desire to make aggressions on any one of these states. On the contrary, it will submit to much from them without showing resentment. If any great civilized power, Russia or Germany, for instance, had behaved toward us as Venezuela under [President Cipriano] Castro behaved, this country would have gone to war at once. We did not go to war with Venezuela merely because our people declined to be irritated by the actions of a weak opponent, and showed a forbearance which probably went beyond the limits of wisdom in refusing to take umbrage at what was done by the weak; although we would certainly have resented it had it been done by the strong. In the case of two states, however, affairs reached such a crisis that we had to act. These two states were Santo Domingo and the then owner of the Isthmus of Panama, Colombia.

Theodore Roosevelt, *Theodore Roosevelt: An Autobiography*. New York: Scribner's, 1913, pp. 506–507.

of Dominican bonds held by New York investors. Roosevelt decided to ignore the Senate's action and signed an executive agreement with the Santo Domingo government that gave him the authority to run the customs houses as he wished. Executive agreements were not new in American diplomacy; a precedent had been set in 1817 when the Rush-Bagot pact between the United States and Great Britain demilitarized the American-Canadian boundary along the Great Lakes. But Roosevelt was going beyond the 1817 precedent by defying and then circumventing the Senate's constitutional power to approve or reject treaties. The Rough Rider nevertheless was building better than even he could have imagined. By 1972 Presidents had so well learned Roosevelt's lesson that executive agreements had largely replaced treaties in American diplomacy; the United States was signatory to 947 treaties, but 4,359 executive agreements. As Roosevelt expanded U.S. power further into the Caribbean, he consolidated diplomatic authority in the White House.

The Roosevelt Corollary

The second important part of Roosevelt's action involved a fundamental redefinition of how the Monroe Doctrine related to U.S. defense. In November 1984, Secretary of Defense Caspar Weinberger appeared on cable television and used the Monroe Doctrine to justify the [Ronald] Reagan administration's policies in Central America. In reality, Weinberger was referring not to the original Monroe Doctrine, but to the transformed and greatly expanded "Roosevelt Corollary" to the Monroe Doctrine, as historians have termed it. Monroe's Doctrine and Roosevelt's Corollary were actually quite different. Monroe sympathized with Latin American revolutions. Roosevelt (and the Reagan administration) opposed such upheavals to the point of being willing to use military force to destroy them. Monroe declared that all nations, including the

United States, should refrain from intervening in the internal affairs of those Latin American states. Roosevelt (and the Reagan administration) justified the use of direct U.S. intervention in Latin American affairs. Monroe did not seize the war-declaring or related powers from Congress, because he had no intention of going to war or even temporarily intervening. Roosevelt (and the Reagan administration) acted on the belief that the chief executive had the right to support the use of United States force (in Reagan's case covert as well as overt), regardless of congressional opposition. In Roosevelt's policy toward Santo Domingo, the United States formally redefined its right to act, militarily if necessary and at the president's sole discretion if the Senate balked, in the internal affairs of Latin American states. Roosevelt's (and the Reagan administration's) actions had little to do with the original Monroe Doctrine, but much to do with the post-1898 view of what constituted the common defense in the United States.

Empowering the Presidency

To defend the new, global American interests, Roosevelt built on McKinley's precedents to create a more centralized and powerful presidency. He placed power above law, although he usually did so with more caution than some scholars have thought. In separating Panama from Colombia in 1903 and taking over the Santo Domingo customs houses in 1904–1905, he nevertheless removed the "constitutional lion in the path"[1] through sheer force. Roosevelt agreed with his friend [Alfred Thayer] Mahan, who had written in 1897 that "men are apt to forget that law is the servant of equity, and that while the world is in its present stage of development equity which cannot be had by law

---

1. A phrase coined by Alfred Thayer Mahan to describe constitutional impediments to America's efforts to secure and protect foreign markets by means of military force.

must be had by force, upon which ultimately law rests, not for its sanction, but for its efficacy." The two men also agreed that neither Congress not [sic] public opinion was well fitted to determine foreign policy. "I can conceive few more pitiful sensations than that of fretting about what the public thinks," Mahan told a friend in 1898, for in "current questions of the day" the public was "a good deal of a fool." Roosevelt put it more delicately when he considered that his policies might be moving against public opinion: "This people of ours simply does not understand how things are outside our own boundaries." As for Congress, it "in the nature of things can know nothing whatever of the totally different conditions of India, or the Philippines, or Egypt, or Cuba . . ." Theodore Roosevelt believed in a "stewardship theory" that assumed the president could take any action he deemed necessary to the general welfare and common defense unless it was expressly forbidden by the Constitution or Congress. As already noted, he was not always willing to abide even by congressionally imposed limits. Given both the new world into which the United States was moving and the latitude offered presidential initiative by McKinley's and Roosevelt's expansion of the commander-in-chief clause of the Constitution, the stewardship theory justified historic centralization of decision-making power. Nor was it simply a temporary, emergency centralization, as had occurred with Andrew Jackson's assumption of power to block South Carolina nullification or Lincoln's breathtaking view of presidential authority in 1861. After 1898, the centralization was becoming systematic, institutionalized, and long-lasting. . . .

The new U.S. foreign policy of 1898 to 1905 transformed the nation's conception of the common defense. That post-1898 turn culminated a long post–Civil War change in United States economic power and the nature of the country's expansion from a quest for territories to a search for overseas markets, preferably of the stable, nonrevolutionary variety. The new type of expansionism and internal consolidation (exemplified by the growth of the corporation and the post-1897 merger movement) had not been accompanied by marked centralization of political power until McKinley entered the White House. His talents and willingness to seize the opportunities offered presidential prerogative by the country's movement into the Caribbean and western Pacific-Asian theaters created an explicit extracontinental definition of the common defense. Overseas expansion and the McKinley-Roosevelt development of presidential power removed the "constitutional lion in the path" that Mahan had feared would stop necessary overseas American expansion. New, centralized powers emerged, powers . . . exercised most notably by McKinley in dispatching troops to China in 1900, and by Roosevelt when he ordered U.S. naval units to put down revolutionary disturbances in Santo Domingo and then control the major source of the country's revenue. Wilson followed these precedents in 1914 when he sent an army into Mexico despite the Senate's refusal to give its consent. Wilson had earlier clearly explained how an expanded overseas empire and centralized political power were coming to work in tandem. His successors, both in academia and in Washington policy-making circles, were to spend the twentieth century trying to control—or, more often, to expand—the awesome power inherent in that partnership.

Roosevelt's Intervention in Panama Was Ethical and Justifiable

Frederick W. Marks III

Many historians have characterized Theodore Roosevelt's foreign policy style as aggressive. Frederick W. Marks III suggests that this conclusion is misguided and ignores the fact that Roosevelt's foreign policy decisions were informed by a sense of moral purpose. Writing about the American intervention that led to the nation's involvement in the construction of the Panama Canal, Marks concludes that the president's sense of justice and honor was a major factor in the decision to undertake the project. Specifically, Marks contends that American action was justified because Colombia went back on its word by rejecting an important treaty. Marks is the author of an important book on Roosevelt's foreign policy: *Velvet on Iron: The Diplomacy of Theodore Roosevelt.*

ALTHOUGH HE CONSISTENTLY INVOKED A HIGHER LAW AND expressed himself in the language of ethics, there is a tendency for historians to discount Roosevelt the moralist and to concentrate instead on Roosevelt the warrior. Scholars have emphasized his spectacular use of power and the oft-repeated words, "Speak softly and carry a big stick." Richard Hofstadter spoke of his "worship of strength," and

Thomas Bailey referred to him as "an apostle of Mars."
Whenever notice is taken of his preaching, the assumption
is apt to be that it was either hypocritical or blindly "self-
righteous." To some students, he appears authoritarian, to
others highhanded. He has been accused of refusing to
meet an opponent halfway and of reacting paranoically to
opposition. According to Bailey, he browbeat other nations
into submission, "especially the smaller ones." According to
Eugene Trani, he deemed "any war in which Americans
fought" to be "just." Howard Beale goes so far as to say that
Roosevelt was convinced that "his country could never act
unjustly or wrongly" and that "when his pride was aroused
or his will crossed," he reacted "like a child determined to
have his own way." If America "could not get what she wanted and do as she pleased without war, then she must fight."

Such charges, usually made *en passant*, are unfortunate. They overlook the complexity of Roosevelt's thought
and ignore a large body of contradictory evidence. But
more important, they conceal the fact that T.R.'s moralistic
approach to international relations requires a rethinking of
the traditional interpretation of "Big Stick" diplomacy, especially with regard to such controversial episodes as the
acquisition of the [Panama] Canal Zone and the settlement of the Alaskan boundary dispute. Although it is impossible to "prove" motivation, it can be shown that Roosevelt was prone by instinct to approach issues in terms of
right and wrong and that he was just as much of a preach-
er as Woodrow Wilson. His preaching may have con-
formed to the spirit of the age and added much to his popular appeal, but it is hard to avoid the conclusion that he
preached with genuine conviction. In addition, his view of
the major events of his administration is worth taking into
serious account if for no other reason than the fact that
there was usually a substantial basis for it. . . .

[The President's] insistence on the binding nature of
even informal agreements sometimes led him to do things

that might appear inexplicable under normal circumstances. Take, for example, the way in which he acquired the Panama Canal Zone—one of the most heavily criticized moves in the annals of American diplomacy. Failing, in sustained effort, to obtain the Zone by treaty with Colombia, he used force to prevent Colombian suppression of an isthmian revolt and proceeded to negotiate directly with the newborn republic, leaving Colombia in a state of impotent rage. Descriptions range all the way from "rape of Colombia" to "cowboy diplomacy." Even [historian] Samuel Flagg Bemis, never one to dwell upon the negative side of American history, calls this "the one really black mark in the Latin American policy of the United States, and a big black mark." Almost every account of the incident stresses Roosevelt's "Big Stick" philosophy and maintains that the Colombians had every right to disapprove their treaty with the United States; that they were at a distinct disadvantage in a contest of strength with their northern neighbor; and that Roosevelt's personal prestige as well as the national interest was tied to the speedy acquisition of a canal zone at Panama. Only a few critics have taken the president at his word when he described the basis for his action as one of high moral principle.

Roosevelt's case is an interesting one, however. To begin with, it was well known at the time that the province of Panama had never been fully integrated into the workings of the Colombian government. It had always conducted its own postal relations with the outside world and never adopted the national paper money, preferring to rely on silver specie. Nor had Panama always been a province of Colombia. When it first obtained independence from Spain in 1821, it established its own government. Thereafter, it voluntarily entered the Granadian Confederation which in 1832 broke apart to form Equador, Venezuela, and New Granada (Colombia). Panama remained with New Granada until 1840, when she resumed independent status. From

1842 to 1855, she was again with the larger state. In 1855, the national constitution was amended to divide power more evenly between central government and provinces, and three subsequent constitutions adopted with the approval of Panama allowed still more local control. Panama thus existed as a virtually sovereign state in confederation with others for twenty-three years until in 1886 her legislature, along with the legislatures of other provinces, was abolished by decree of Bogotá, and she was summarily stripped of nearly all her autonomy. The two Panamanian delegates who attended the constitutional convention of 1886 were both appointed by Bogotá, and neither had ever lived in Panama. Nor was the new instrument of government ever submitted for approval to the Panamanian people.

With three-quarters of the people reportedly in favor of separation, the year 1885 saw the outbreak of the first in a series of three full-scale insurrections which led eventually to complete independence. Twice, the people fought to exhaustion only to be put down by United States marines. In the rising of 1901–1902, they outnumbered their opponents on the isthmus by seven thousand to four thousand and had routed them in battle before American forces intervened to frustrate their bid for final victory. The revolution of 1903 was therefore the third major effort on the part of the Panamanian patriots. It was also a revolution which, by democratic standards, had every right to succeed, since the relationship between central government and province had always been one of exploitation rather than of reciprocal benefit. For decades, Colombian politicians had derived a good portion of the national revenue from isthmian railway tolls without returning a pittance for the building of schools, hospitals, and other public facilities. President [José M.] Marroquín's apparent willingness to gamble with the economic future of the isthmus by trying to squeeze the United States and the New Panama Canal Company was thus only one more grievance on a list of many.

It should also be recalled that even in physical terms Bogotá was separated from the isthmus by impassable jungle and awesome mountain terrain. At an altitude of 8,700 feet, the capital could not be reached from the sea in less than twelve days, three by mule and nine by rail. Provincials could make the trip to Washington, D.C., more quickly than they could arrive at the seat of their own government.

Order Through Power

Theodore Roosevelt biographer John Morton Blum sees consistency in the president's approach to Latin America. Roosevelt was convinced, Blum thinks, that order could be achieved in Latin America through the use of U.S. power. The president was following through with his intentions when he aided the Panamanian revolt and gained control of the canal zone.

Insistence upon order in areas of strategic significance had provided Roosevelt, before he announced his corollary to the Monroe Doctrine, with a warrant for acquiring the canal zone in Panama. Long convinced that an isthmian canal was indispensable for American naval policy, persuaded by the report of the second Walker Commission that Panama was the preferred site for this canal, he had no patience with Colombia's rejection of the treaty providing a suitable right of way. He planned before the Panamanian revolt against Colombia to seize what he desired. For this plan he had prepared an apologia, perhaps compelling and certainly convenient. He used it to justify the course he ultimately took. When in 1903 the Panamanians declared their independence, Roosevelt saw to it that American forces aided the revolt. He at once recognized the new republic. Without this collaboration it could not have long survived. In return he received the controversial right of way, control over the zone through which the United States constructed the canal.

Disorder in so vital an area as the isthmus, Roosevelt

[Secretary of War] Elihu Root summed up the ethical issue when he pointed out that a strong Colombia had long held a weak Panama "in unlawful subjection," and Roosevelt was able to note in his Annual Address of 1903 that Panama had experienced fifty-three outbreaks, rebellions, and revolutionary disturbances in the fifty-three years since the United States had agreed to guarantee free

then declared as he had planned to, had made essential his treatment of Colombia: "The experience of over half a century has shown Colombia to be utterly incapable of keeping order on the Isthmus . . . The control, in the interest of the commerce and traffic of the whole civilized world, of the means of undisturbed transit across the Isthmus of Panama has become of transcendent importance to the United States. We have repeatedly exercised this control by intervening in the course of domestic dissension . . . the goverment of Colombia, though wholly unable to maintain order on the Isthmus, has nevertheless declined to ratify a treaty the conclusion of which opened the only chance to secure its own stability and to guarantee permanent peace on, and the construction of a canal across, the Isthmus." Under these circumstances, he averred, the United States had no choice but to aid the revolution. This reasoning was not merely a cloak for grabbing land. In what he did, certainly in the way he did it, Roosevelt was wrong; but he was also convinced and consistent. In Panama as in Cuba and Santo Domingo, he used power to establish order. Had he been elected President in 1912, in order to protect American lives and property he would "have restored order in Mexico, if necessary at the cost of war."

This was imperialism—about that there can be no argument.

John Morton Blum, *The Republican Roosevelt*, 2nd ed. Cambridge, MA: Harvard University Press, 1977.

and open transit across the isthmus. In addition, it is clear that the Colombian government had requested the aid of American troops to enforce order on the isthmus at least six different times (Roosevelt mentioned only four).

At the very time the treaty talks were taking place, American marines were again in Panama on behalf of a Colombian dictator engulfed in the worst civil war of his nation's history and threatened with invasion by Venezuela. It would have been easy to take advantage of the situation, especially since the Panamanian rebels promised a liberal canal treaty. Nevertheless, Secretary of State [John] Hay sustained negotiations with Colombia for over two years until the dictator, José Marroquín, triumphed over all his rivals. Several times during this period, Hay reluctantly agreed to pay higher sums of money for a treaty which included such minimum security provisions as control of local police and establishment of American courts. The Colombian minister to the United States had been instructed to accept all of Hay's terms except those relating to price. Money was therefore the main stumbling block at the beginning, as it was to be at the end.

The crux of the issue for both Roosevelt and Hay was the expectation that once Marroquín had committed himself to the treaty as the best obtainable in competition with Nicaragua, he would be honor-bound to recommend it to his countrymen. Technically, Colombia had the right to reject the treaty, since it was a sovereign state with a constitution requiring congressional approval under normal conditions. But the canal negotiations had been initiated by Colombia. Three Colombian ministers had urged the treaty upon the United States for two years. The United States had agreed to purchase the rights and property of the French New Panama Canal Company with the express consent of Colombia, which held one million francs' worth of stock in the company, and whose representative at a stockholders' meeting had voted accordingly. It was on such assurances that the United States had concluded its agreement with the French company and that Congress had reversed itself, under strong administration pressure, from its original decision to designate Nicaragua as the preferred site. Thus, as Hay indicated to the Colombian minister of foreign affairs, "the United States, in view of the foregoing facts and of the responsibilities which it has thus been induced to incur, considers that the pending treaty is in the nature of a conclusive agreement on the part of Colombia." Marroquín's support was, in other words, not only something that had been promised, but also a "warrantable expectation."

In actual fact, Marroquín acted from the moment the treaty was signed to mobilize opinion against it. He not only failed to endorse it in his New Year's Message of 1903 but encouraged open debate, saying he would let the masses decide. General Fernandez, minister of finance, issued a circular to the Bogotá press inviting public discussion and reaffirming that the government "had no preconceived wishes for or against." One of Marroquín's more obvious moves was to solicit the opinion of three well-known lawyers, who responded with a uniformly critical view. Certainly, for the victor of a Latin-American civil war that had claimed over one hundred and fifty thousand lives, this was tantamount to inviting the treaty's defeat. The British minister to Bogotá observed that "the measures employed by the Colombian government to prevent public discussion of affairs of state [over a period of many years] have had the effect of destroying anything like public opinion." And he was correct. What passed for "public opinion," said to be enthusiastic at first, now shifted quickly to the negative. The Marroquín government continued to claim that it had no feelings for or against the treaty, while the American minister in Bogotá reported nothing but criticism coming from a press which he described as having "suddenly sprung into existence." He could not find a single journal or newspaper willing to publish an article in favor of the treaty, even though the articles that did appear gave no hint of Nicaraguan competition in the bidding and ridiculously exaggerated the profits expected to accrue to the United States.

Double-Dealing or Diplomacy?

Equally significant is the fact that when the time arrived to elect delegates for a congress specially called to consider the treaty (and the first to meet since 1898), the governor of Panama, who was a Marroquín appointee, named an antitreaty man as government candidate for the congress. This individual was then declared elected, despite the fact that the overwhelming sentiment in the province of Panama favored the treaty.

Historians have claimed that Marroquín was not to blame because he was politically weak. But the truth of the matter was well put by the Colombian consul in New York, who insisted that there was no party in Colombia "strong enough to defeat the wishes of the President." As soon as the congress convened, Marroquín showed himself firmly in control by mustering a vote of thirty-eight to five against an opposition party motion demanding to see all executive correspondence on the treaty. Marroquín supporters were elected president and vice-president of the senate, and the government went on to carry every important question in the course of the debate. Secretary Hay suspected that Marroquín might submit the treaty without recommendation. But the Colombian president went considerably beyond this to stall the proceedings and pave the way for the treaty's defeat should the United States refuse to pay large additional sums of money. In his opening address, he announced that he would only suggest that Colombia was in a good position to demand better terms. He withheld the treaty for several weeks and then cavalierly submitted it without his signature, an act unprecedented in Colombian history. Two weeks of debate thus revolved around the question of whether congress had the right to consider an unsigned document. In the meantime, he sought additional sums from representatives of both the United States and the French Panama Canal Company, intimating that this was the only way to ensure senate approval.

Mysterious things happened. There was a secret meeting on 30 June between the senate and Marroquín's foreign minister at which he revealed a strongly worded plea from the United States. There was also an unusual failure of telegraph service for three critical weeks during which a senate committee decided to attach nine amendments to the treaty, including a stipulation for more money. On 4 August, the committee issued its report; on 5 August, telegraph service resumed, and the American minister was presented with an urgent and long-delayed wire from Hay. Other cables were unaccountably lost.

In the end, Marroquín's special congress voted unanimously to reject the treaty, and the Panamanians carried out their long-threatened revolt. Bogotá failed to send early reinforcements, despite Roosevelt's frank warning that in such a situation he would avail himself of his legal right to maintain peace along the Panama railroad and prevent all troops from landing within a radius of fifty miles. Four hundred of Marroquín's troops did manage to land at Colón before Roosevelt acted, but they could do little on their own and were actually saved from an encounter with eager Panamanian forces nearly four times as large when the American naval commander refused them access to Panama City.

The Colombian government now asked for American aid in putting down the revolt and offered, in return, to approve the ill-fated [U.S.-Colombian] Hay-Herrán Treaty either by presidential decree or by summoning an extra session of congress with new and friendly members. This only confirmed T.R.'s suspicions of double-dealing and steeled him all the more in his support of Panamanian independence. It is unnecessary to recall the long history of Panamanian separatism, the periods when the province had enjoyed various degrees of autonomy, or the many times Colombian authorities had been unable to put down insurrection on the isthmus without American aid. Suffice to say that in the opinion of both Hay and Roosevelt, a failure to intervene would have resulted in "endless guerrilla warfare." Hay had advised Roosevelt that we "shall be forced" to do something "in the case of a serious insurrectionary movement in Panama to keep the transit clear. Our intervention should not be haphazard, nor this time should it be to the profit, as heretofore, of Bogotá." And the president, for his part, harbored a fear of intervention by some European power and appreciated his responsibility to protect the lives of American citizens.

Even more to the point, the issue was conceived in terms of moral principle. Roosevelt might have shifted the negotiations to Nicaragua; he might have discouraged revolutionary sentiment on the isthmus; he might even have helped Colombia put the revolution down. But, apart from political and practical considerations, such actions would have been entirely out of character. It would have earned him, in his own words, a place in Dante's inferno "beside the faint-hearted cleric who was guilty of *il gran rifiuto* [the great refusal]." Marroquín's last-minute demands for more money struck him as outrageous, and he filled his personal correspondence with words such as "homicidal corruptionists," "extortion," and "blackmail." Marroquín, an absolute dictator with power to "keep his promise or break it," had "determined to break it." The Colombian congress was an assembly "of mere puppets," a "sham," and the country "had forfeited every claim to consideration." Nor was that "stating the case strongly enough; she had so acted that yielding to her would have meant on our part that culpable form of weakness which stands on a level with wickedness."

Roosevelt's Panamanian Policy Was Defined by Aggression and Contradiction

David H. Burton

Historian David H. Burton argues that highly personal motives, including both ambition and a desire to improve the world, often drove Theodore Roosevelt's foreign policy decisions. These impulses often led to aggressive and contradictory actions. Burton suggests that Roosevelt's aggressiveness and conflicting values can be seen especially in the case of his policy regarding the Panama Canal. Burton is the author of *Theodore Roosevelt: Confident Imperialist.*

C HRONOLOGICALLY SPEAKING, IT WAS THE FIRST INSTANCE of aggressive Rooseveltian diplomacy—the acquisition of canal rights in Panama—that stands as the best single example of the positive and negative effects of United States policy in Central American affairs. In the "taking of Panama" virtually every element in Theodore Roosevelt's conception of and contribution to the world move-

Excerpted from *Theodore Roosevelt: Confident Imperialist*, by David H. Burton (Philadelphia: University of Pennsylvania Press, 1968). Copyright © 1968 by University of Pennsylvania Press. All rights reserved. Reprinted with permission.

ment[1] stands out. Because of his highly personal and unusually decisive part in the Panama episode, it may be said
to summarize various conflicting ingredients that must be
placed in relationship one to another in evaluating Roosevelt's world movement frame of reference. Some of these
elements were not easily reconciled. In theory probably
there can be no satisfactory resolution of them. Yet Big
Stick, and therefore United States, diplomacy over a number of years were both based on such a set of principles
with divergent values. This indicates that in a particular
crisis a collision of principles can be avoided by a states-
man's response to the exigencies of a given moment. The
progression of events resolves at the time and for the time
being the inconsistencies upon which policy may be based,
inconsistencies that in the case of the acquisition of canal
rights in Panama were no more forgivable by opponents
critical of the action than they were admissible by Roosevelt years after the events had taken place.

To Construct a Canal

As was typical of the leading issues early in his Administration, Roosevelt did not inherit in Panama a general condition that he was relatively free to act upon, but a defined
policy that already had received some implementation
under President [William] McKinley. As McKinley's successor and as a Republican President, he was to a degree
committed to his predecessor's intentions to construct a
canal somewhere in Central America.

Roosevelt personally was strongly in favor of the canal
undertaking. Years before, in 1894, he had linked United
States construction of an Isthmian canal to the right and
necessity of national expansion into the Pacific. Samoa,

---

1. Roosevelt's vision of a new U.S. imperialism characterized by helping bring order to
world affairs and helping undeveloped countries grow to embrace democratic ideals

Hawaii, a great navy, and a canal—these were all crucial to America's world position, and he wished his Republican Party would build the canal "with the money of Uncle Sam." The Spanish War intensified interest in the prospect of an American-sponsored canal, and Roosevelt with his special concern for the Navy and his sense of naval strategy as it affected national prestige wanted to be sure that if such a canal was built it would be fortified by the United States rather than in some manner internationalized. He told Albert Shaw that a canal was not enough, only a fortified canal would serve American interests. "Better have no canal at all than not give us the power to control it in time of war," he wrote.

In the amplification of his canal views Roosevelt tended to emphasize several large considerations. First among them was the Monroe Doctrine. "If Germany has the same right we have in the canal across Central America," he observed to John Hay in expressing his unqualified disapproval of the first Hay-Pauncefote agreement [between the United States and Great Britain], "then why not in the partition of any part of South America? . . . If we invite foreign powers to a joint ownership or a joint guarantee of what so vitally concerns us . . . how can we possibly object to similar joint action say in Southern Brazil . . .?" A second strategic aspect of the canal enterprise was the solidification of Anglo-American friendship that would no doubt result. In Roosevelt's opinion "it is really for England's interest that America should fortify the canal," thus relieving the British of military responsibilities in the Western Hemisphere at a time when her world position faced the new German challenge. A greater identity of the superior Anglo-American peoples with each other was completely consistent with Roosevelt's historical premises, and when circumstances promoted what he accounted mutual advantage for England and the United States he very willingly lent his support. Roosevelt also chose to see the canal in terms of the ultimate purpose of the world movement—the betterment of mankind that could be expected from it—though at first he was inclined to stress this as resulting from the promotion of American national interest.

Two Possible Routes

Britain's formal acquiescence in the United States' intention to build an Isthmian canal made determination of the route the waterway would take the next step. Two routes were under serious consideration by the United States at the time. One was across Nicaragua, where the presence of natural lakes promised to facilitate the construction, and the other was in Panama, where a French company had tried and failed to link the two great oceans of the world. Roosevelt was especially concerned about doing the politically correct thing. Though he was not against a Nicaraguan canal in principle, he was aware that the weight of engineering opinion favored the Panama route, and to him this figured as a very important plus factor for that route. His respect for expert engineering judgment was reinforced by his desire to avoid a disaster at the canal site and harm to his political career. With congressional approval of a canal across Panama (the Spooner Act, June 1902) the President was anxious to complete arrangements for construction in that area. Panama or Nicaragua? The important thing was to make the dirt fly.

Anticipating a successful arrangement with Colombia for Isthmian rights, the President in his second annual message to Congress played up the positive aspects of a great canal, linking human betterment with national advantage. "The Canal will be of great benefit to America and of importance to all the world," he declared. "It will be of advantage to us industrially and also as improving our military position. It will be of advantage to the countries of tropical America. . . . It will invite to their shores commerce and improve their material conditions by recognizing that stability and order are prerequisites of successful development."

Trouble with the Talks

Unhappily, the negotiations between the United States and Colombia ran a troubled course from the start. Talks between Dr. [José] Concha, the Colombian minister in Washington, and Secretary Hay had begun as early as March, at a time when Congress was still debating the choice of routes. Roosevelt was in almost constant contact with Hay and thus knew daily the frustrations attendant upon Concha's refusal to accept American terms. "Terms" rather than "proposals" better describes the tone of the American attitude. Perhaps these frustrations experienced by men bargaining from a position of strength contributed to Roosevelt's determination to take Panama. Diplomatic decisions of great moment are not of necessity insulated from such personal factors.

American demands upon the Colombians were far-reaching. The United States insisted that Colombia renounce its sovereignty over a canal zone. This was the principal and most onerous proposal. In addition, however, Colombia was to be prohibited from dealing with the French company, the New Panama Canal Company as it was called, for cancellation of concessions previously granted. In return for these accommodations the United States agreed to pay an indemnity of $10,000,000, along with annual payments of $250,000. Dr. Concha considered the monetary arrangements grossly inadequate when compared with the surrenders of principle and territory asked of his country, for what the United States was seeking was no less than an infringement of Colombian sovereignty.

Only after months of conversations, during which Concha himself withdrew in protest over the American attitude, was an agreement of sorts reached. Concha had left Tomas Herran, the Colombian chargé in Washington, to continue representations to the State Department. When Hay informed the Bogotá government on December 30, 1902, that the United States intended to switch to a Nicaraguan canal, the pressure was sufficient to bring about agreement. The Hay-Herran Convention, granting the United States demands, was signed on January 22, 1903, and approved by the American Senate the following March 17. Thereafter the fate of the treaty rested with Bogotá.

The Colombian Government, in the hands of President [José M.] Marroquin, a dictator who had come to power by a *coup d'état* in 1898, was opposed to the terms of the Hay-Herran Convention from the outset. Dispatches sent by the American minister at Bogotá, A.M. Beaupré, leave no doubt on this score, portraying the source of Colombian opposition as national pride rather than personal greed. Marroquin convened a special session of the Colombian congress, which he had hitherto ignored, to consider the treaty. The congress merely became an additional source of virulent opposition to the proposed accord. The United States Government for its part was adamant and unyielding in its position; any change whatsoever in the provisions that Bogotá might suggest would be construed as a sign of bad faith and would be summarily rejected by Washington. If, as Roosevelt claimed, he was in direct, personal charge of guiding American policy toward Colombia during these months he must be held responsible for the unrelenting pressure brought upon the smaller nation and the highhanded manner of its execution. Despite this American insistence and Theodore Roosevelt to the contrary, the Colombian congress rejected the treaty on August 12. Events had now placed the American Government in a quandary. Secretary Hay advised the President that two courses of action remained open to the United States: reactivation of a Nicaraguan canal project or construction in Panama regardless of Colombia.

The Right of Way

Meanwhile, in August, about the same time the treaty was rejected at Bogotá, Roosevelt was shown a memorandum written by John Bassett Moore, a professor of international law at Columbia University and himself a former Assistant Secretary of State. Acting Secretary of State F.B. Loomis was instrumental in placing the Moore critique before the President. Roosevelt read Moore's statement with consuming interest. It was Moore's professional opinion that an old (1846) treaty between the United States and New Granada (Colombia), guaranteeing to the United States "the right of way in transit across the Isthmus of Panama upon any modes of communication that now exist, or that may be hereafter constructed, shall be free and open to the Government and citizens of the United States," still carried weight.

While Professor Moore, reflecting the caution of his craft, contended only that this old treaty provided grounds for a serious continuation of negotiations, to Roosevelt it meant much more than that. It meant that the United States already had sufficient legal grounds to warrant action in the name of a Panama canal. "If under the Treaty of 1846 we have a color of right to start in and build the canal," he confided to Hay, "my off-hand judgment would favor such proceedings. It seems that the great bulk of the best engineers are agreed that that route is the best, and I do not think that the Bogotá lot of jack rabbits should be allowed permanently to bar one of the future highways of civilization."

It is doubtful that the Moore memorandum and a subsequent meeting with Moore at Sagamore Hill in mid-September had yet convinced the President finally of the line of action to be taken; events had not as yet progressed so far. On September 10, for example, he told Jacob Gould Schurman of his canal dilemma. He admitted his fear that any public statement on his part "would undoubtedly be taken as equivalent to an effort to incite [in Panama] an insurrection" favorable to American ambitions. But he added he would "infinitely prefer to get title to the Canal outright" and did not "consent for one moment to the view that Colombia had the right permanently to block one of the world's great highways." Perhaps he hesitated in his decision because of his agreement with Schurman "that to wait a few months, or even a year or two, is nothing compared with having the thing done rightly."

The Course of Events

A week later, on the day of his meeting with Moore, he [Roosevelt] was still inclined to wonder which canal should be built. "No one can tell what will come out in the Isthmian Canal business," he observed to [William Howard] Taft. "This winter we may start the Nicaraguan Canal, or the *course of events* may force us to take action in Panama." A letter to Hay dated the same day, September 15, added further claim to his indecision, just as it left undisputed his contempt for the Bogotá Government. "At present I feel there are two alternatives. (1) To take up Nicaragua; (2) in some shape or way to interfere when it becomes necessary so as to secure the Panama route without further dealing with the foolish and homicidal corruptionists in Bogotá." The overtones of these confidences to Taft and Hay are remarkably indicative of the President's willingness to keep his policy flexible enough to be able to respond most advantageously to a developing situation.

With no small amount of assistance from the Panama conspirators "the course of events" took a fortuitous turn: revolution in Panama against Colombian authority. The conspiracy, dominated at this stage by [Philippe] Bunau-Varilla, had no official assurances from Washington that the United States would support an uprising at the Isthmus, a *coup* that would have as its objective an independent Republic of Panama free to deal directly with the American Government regarding canal rights.

Neither did the conspirators receive any discouragement of their plans. In a conversation with the President, Bunau-Varilla heard from the Chief Executive such extreme expressions of hostility toward Colombia that he could not and did not assume that the United States would allow a Panama revolution to fail. Furthermore, the President ordered the U.S.S. *Marblehead*, the U.S.S. *Dixie*, and the U.S.S. *Nashville* into the waters around the Isthmus to prevent any hostile force from occupying Panama. The legal basis of his instructions to his naval commanders was the provision of the Treaty of 1846 guaranteeing the "perfect neutrality" of the Isthmus. American forces successfully "neutralized" the area to the distinct benefit of the revolutionaries when the time was appropriate.

The nature and extent of Roosevelt's complicity in these swiftly moving events, however, is less germane than his reasons for acting or not acting. As the rebels made their preparations, in which Roosevelt apparently had no direct part, he repudiated either bribery or violence, as means unworthy of American ambitions in Central America. But he was hemmed in by events, specifically the refusal of the Colombian Government to accede to American demands. A Nicaraguan canal was against the advice of the great majority of competent engineers, he complained at the time, leaving the United States little practical choice but to move in the direction events would take in Panama. His official inaction, of course, helped to control these events while a formal pose of neutrality if not disinterest was maintained.

Roosevelt's World Outlook

Roosevelt's ambiguous posture can be explained in terms of the conflicting elements in his world outlook: A nation, like an individual, must bear witness to the right; at the same time, law and order had to be observed and human betterment promoted. The benevolent Roosevelt and the ambitious Roosevelt were at odds once again. Events served to resolve this conflict. The interests of civilization must take precedence over those of "the little wildcat republic of Colombia [because it] behaved infamously about the treaty for the building of the Panama Canal." The Colombians had forfeited their right to civilized consideration because of their inferiority as a people. Roosevelt pronounced them "not merely corrupt" but "governmentally utterly incompetent." Their inferiority was all the more unfortunate because their corruption and incompetence stood in the way of a great human achievement—the canal. The President's mood of frustration can be gauged tolerably well by his denunciation of those who dared oppose him at this time as "shrill eunuchs."

Roosevelt matched the march of events in Panama stride for stride. The revolution began on November 3, 1903 under the guns of American warships; the next day Panama declared itself an independent republic. The American Government at the direction of the President extended diplomatic recognition with uncommon haste (on November 6). By the 18th of the month an appropriate treaty had been drawn up committing Panama to United States canal requirements; approval by the American Senate came on February 23, 1904. Roosevelt defended these moves as "justified by the interests of collective civilization" inasmuch as the United States held a "mandate" from mankind to construct an interoceanic waterway. In explaining matters to [Cecil] Spring-Rice he conveniently lumped together American national interest, the welfare of the people at the Isthmus as well as of all mankind, the benefits to law and order, and the political incapacity of the "Bogotá bandits" as the circumstances encouraging the United States to let events occur as they would. He might well have added his determination to enter the presidential race with arrangements to build an American canal completed, for undoubtedly his political ambitions were a vital ingredient in his total policy. Any one of these considerations would have provided sufficient warrant in his judgment to proceed in Panama; combined, they enabled Roosevelt to defend his policy as not merely necessary but virtuous.

The President undertook a full-dress defense of his handling of United States-Colombian relations in his third annual message. Although much of what he said was a review of happenings, beginning as far back as Colombian independence, certain of his arguments merit brief mention: As policeman of the hemisphere the United States by treaty right and by precedent was responsible for the neutrality of the Isthmus. The failure of the Colombian Government to ratify a treaty made by an official of that Government was evidence of the perfidy of the Colombians and of their incapacity to conduct political affairs with other nations in a proper way. The enormous benefit to the world that an Isthmian canal would bring about made it incumbent upon the United States to undertake the project. Equally compelling was American self-interest. Here was the official apologia, an in-depth defense of American canal diplomacy, the details of which were subsumed by the world movement patterns of Roosevelt's thought.

No doubt Theodore Roosevelt acted as he had in the canal crisis in response to a developing situation. And one can be equally sure he saw in the results of his practical policy the first steps of a great human undertaking bound to effect the betterment of nations and people. As far as his own country was concerned he believed the building of the canal would "rank in kind, though not of course in degree, with the Louisiana Purchase and the acquisition of Texas." In attempting to understand the influence of the world movement on Roosevelt's policy in Panama, or elsewhere in the Caribbean for that matter, it must be kept in mind that his was a highly personalized appraisal of what would serve the world best. This concept of the world movement was less a doctrine to believe in, which others could discern as an objective norm for action, and more a personal way of looking at things, an evaluation of what the situation demanded that was substantially in keeping with one or several of its major propositions. The world movement idea did not shackle Roosevelt in his approach to decision-making. It liberated him by offering him a variety of purposes for acting in the solution of problems that events foisted upon him, answers he was impelled to discover by his own temperament and by his high public office.

PRESIDENTS
and their
DECISIONS

CHAPTER

4

THE GREAT
WHITE FLEET
AND U.S.
NAVAL POWER

Roosevelt Helped to Create a Powerful Navy

Anna K. Nelson

Even as a student, Theodore Roosevelt was interested in naval power. As a young man, he gained literary notoriety for his senior thesis at Harvard—*The Naval War of 1812*—which was published as a book. The author of the following section, Anna K. Nelson, notes that throughout his life Roosevelt advocated the position that national prestige, foreign policy, and power require a strong navy. Even before his presidency, Roosevelt was the foremost champion of the U.S. Navy. He can be credited with developing the "Great White Fleet" that would later allow him to pursue many of his international initiatives as president. Anna K. Nelson is a distinguished historian at American University and the author of several works on American diplomatic history.

A BOUT 50 YEARS AGO, A VERY POPULAR PLAY, *ARSENIC AND Old Lace,* began its long run in American high schools. It was about two elderly ladies who poisoned their elderly gentlemen callers with elderberry wine. Periodically, a clearly manic young man who thought he was Theodore Roosevelt would come on stage with round glasses and mustache, dressed in pith helmet and shorts or army cavalry uniform. He would shout at the top of his lungs, "Charge!," and leap up the stairs, presumably up San

Juan Hill. In spite of the repetition, the line was always good for a laugh.

While this character bore little resemblance to the former president, it does indicate something about public knowledge of Roosevelt's accomplishments. It is ironic that Theodore Roosevelt is so often depicted in an army uniform as the commander of the "Rough Riders" on the landmass of Cuba. Roosevelt was a Navy man. His army career was brief, to say the least, and his real contribution to the Spanish-Cuban-American War went far beyond his celebrated career with the Rough Riders.

Even as a young boy, Teddy Roosevelt was enamored with the Navy. Ships and adventures on the high seas intrigued him. He defied convention by pursuing this interest, and his senior thesis at Harvard, *The Naval War of 1812*, was published in 1882, eight years before Alfred Thayer Mahan published *The Influence of Sea Power Upon History*.

McKinley's Navy Appointee

When the election of 1896 ensured Republican control of both the legislative and executive branches of government, Roosevelt wanted nothing more than to be assistant secretary of the Navy. When his friends, including Senator Henry Cabot Lodge of Massachusetts, approached the newly elected William McKinley, they found him concerned about Roosevelt's bellicose reputation. McKinley explained to them that he wanted a peaceful presidency and feared that Roosevelt's conduct would lead to war.

Finally persuaded that Roosevelt would be a loyal supporter of his administration, McKinley made the appointment. It was a greater opportunity for influence than even Roosevelt had foreseen. His superior, Secretary of the Navy John D. Long, was a man of little energy, who preferred long vacations in New England to working and had lengthy visits with the doctor who took care of the painful corns on his feet. Roosevelt, on the other hand, was a man of prodigious energy who learned more about the inner workings of the U.S. Navy in one week than Long would learn throughout his entire term of office.

Roosevelt set out to build up the Navy and cultivate the powerful people who could influence the passage of large appropriations. Mahan became his collaborator. The officer supplied arguments for Roosevelt, and the latter tried to further Mahan's views by publicizing his articles. Although Alfred Thayer Mahan influenced Roosevelt's views, he was only one of a larger group of influential associates. Before Roosevelt came to office in 1897, he had already aligned himself with a coterie of men, including Henry Cabot Lodge, Brooks Adams, and John Hay, who were devoted to a "larger policy," the overseas expansion of American interests. These men were both intellectually involved in seeking a new American paradigm and politically involved in solving the issues of the day.

Roosevelt and Lodge, for example, were disappointed that Hawaii had yet to be annexed, and exerted their influence to convince McKinley to overcome that deficiency even before the war with Spain. They chafed over public indifference to foreign affairs at a time when all the great powers were carving out empires while the Americans were being left behind. They believed in the superiority of the Anglo-Saxons and took to themselves the responsibility for taking care of "lesser" peoples.

But Roosevelt and his fellow expansionists, unlike their twentieth-century successors, were not concerned with promoting American economic interests. Their primary concern was national power and prestige. "I wish to see the United States the dominant power on the Pacific Ocean," Roosevelt wrote. "Our people are neither craven nor weaklings and we face the future high of heart and confident of soul eager to do the great work of a great power." Consistent with their forbears, they turned to the tradition of "Manifest Destiny" to differentiate their plans for world power from those of the European imperialists.

Observing the success of Great Britain, the growth of Germany, and the increasing dominance of Japan as a Pacific power, the expansionists looked for a common denominator. It was easily found. Strong, imperial powers had large, world-class navies. For the United States to take its proper place in the world, it must also have a great navy. Roosevelt's public explanation was that a large navy would prevent war. He wrote that if the United States built and maintained an "adequate" navy and made it clear that "we are perfectly ready and willing to fight for our rights, then the chances of war will become infinitesimal."

A Man for Peace

But there was a second purpose in Roosevelt's mind. In Howard Beale's words, Roosevelt believed that "the Navy was an instrument of national policies that could not be carried out without it." Roosevelt saw the Navy as a protector, a strategic necessity for an active, great power. He wanted a large navy so that the country could "take the position to which it is entitled among the nations of the earth."

As Assistant Secretary of the Navy, Roosevelt set out to build this impressive navy; a navy strong enough to fight a war, and important enough to make the United States into a world power. McKinley's views notwithstanding, Roosevelt also had a war plan for his navy a year before the war with Spain actually began. His plan would entail a naval blockade of Cuba that would lead to the liberation of Cuba, not its annexation. If necessary, because of the war, the Navy would attack the Philippines. Again the United States would not plan to annex the Philippines, but rather have a "controlling voice." Thus, while Roosevelt's navy was making the United States safe for peace, it was busy preparing for war, a war President McKinley was not eager to declare.

The ink was barely dry on the declaration of war when

Roosevelt the adventurer ordered his uniform from Brooks Brothers and went off to fight against Spain. He acquitted himself splendidly and never forgot the hours he spent on San Juan Hill. Nevertheless, his few months as a cavalryman were of little consequence compared to the impact of a message he sent to the commander of the Asiatic Squadron, Commodore George Dewey. Judging that war would come sooner rather than later, Roosevelt sent Dewey a message that allowed him to move swiftly into Manila Bay once war was declared. Dewey prepared his ships, took on coal, and, when the United States was finally at war, destroyed the Spanish squadron in the Philippines. This move alone was

The Big Stick?

Contrary to Roosevelt's image as a "war hawk" who carried a "big stick," author Martin D. Tullai maintains that the president was committed to the path of peace.

This has become the stereotyped "Man of the Big Stick" image of Theodore Roosevelt—the bellicose, aggressive character ever ready to initiate a conflict. But his famous axiom "Speak softly and carry a big stick, and you will go far," which he constantly advised all who would listen, showed him to be a man who put persuasion before force. The availability of raw power—preparedness—not the use of it made for effective diplomacy. George Washington, incidentally, would have agreed with this view. After all, he once declared, "There is nothing which will so soon produce a speedy and honorable peace as a state of preparation for war."

Significantly, perhaps ironically, Roosevelt was the first American as well as one of only two U.S. presidents to receive the Nobel Peace Prize. This was in 1906 for his mediation in the Russo-Japanese conflict, a mediation that ended war and led to peace. He then donated the entire $40,000 he received to a foundation for the promotion of industrial peace.

a lasting contribution, for better or for worse, of Roosevelt as Assistant Secretary of the Navy.

"America Is Now a Great Power"

In many ways, Roosevelt and the war of 1898 had a kind of symbiotic relationship. The war itself was a result of the efforts of Roosevelt, Lodge, Mahan, and others to send a message to the world, especially Great Britain, that "America is now a great power. Ignore it at your peril." On the other hand, it is doubtful that Roosevelt could have accomplished his goals if there had been no war with Spain. Tensions were growing, the Hearst papers were all but screaming about

---

Yes, he did tell the War College in Newport, Rhode Island, "All the great masterful races have been fighting races; and the minute that a race loses the hard fighting virtues, then . . . it has lost its proud fight to stand as equal of the best."

And yes, he wrote: "The man who fears death more than dishonor, more than failure to perform duty, is a poor citizen; and the nation that regards war as the worst of all evils and the avoidance of war as the highest good is a wretched and contemptible nation, and it is well that it should vanish from the earth."

And yes again, he said: "No triumph of peace is quite as great as the supreme triumph of war."

He also declared: "An ignoble peace is even worse than an unsuccessful war."

Although Roosevelt expressed these views regarding war and indicated that sometimes war is justified, he also said: "I abhor unjust war. I should never advocate war unless it were the only alternative to dishonor. . . . I deplore that the need even for just war should ever occur. . . . Every honorable effort should always be made to avoid war."

Martin D. Tullai, "Theodore Roosevelt: A Man for All Ages," *World & I*, vol. 13, no. 4, April 1998, pp. 327–28.

Spanish brutality, the expansionists were pushing McKinley, and the Cuban "exiles" were not-so-secretly abusing the neutrality acts. Critical of McKinley's unwillingness to declare war to assuage the ills of the Cubans, Roosevelt was convinced that war would ultimately come and that the United States had to be prepared.

The coming war allowed Roosevelt to put the Navy in "good shape." He was able to get the appropriations from Congress and faced no interference from McKinley. Roosevelt firmly believed that the United States must have a great navy to take its place in the world. The war gave Roosevelt the ability to begin building that navy, which, in turn, helped turn the country into a Pacific power.

After a term as Governor of New York, Roosevelt was nominated to be vice president in the election of 1900. In a matter of months, McKinley was dead from an assassin's bullet and Theodore Roosevelt was President of the United States, an accidental president who entered office with strong views concerning the future of the country.

A Two-Ocean Navy

Roosevelt, heir to the heritage of Polk and Seward, always regarded the United States as a Pacific power as well as an Atlantic power. He was impressed by the rapid modernization of Japan and its success in the Sino-Japanese War of 1895. Roosevelt saw Japan as a potential threat to American interests in the Far East (East Asia); hence his message to Dewey and the annexation of the Philippines. Of course the annexation of Hawaii provided the United States with sovereignty over islands far from the nation's shores. But as a mere glance at a map will illustrate, annexing the Philippines moved U.S. strategic interests into the heart of Asia. It was partly to ensure the presence of U.S. interests in the Pacific that Roosevelt sent American battleships around the world, perhaps the best known of his efforts at naval foreign policy. The "Great White Fleet" was impressive, especially when it sailed into Japanese harbors. The Japanese were so impressed they stepped up the building of their own navy.

As president, Roosevelt turned more and more of his attention to Japan. His Nobel Peace Prize came as a result of his role in the Treaty of Portsmouth, which marked the conclusion of the Russo-Japanese War. His mediating hand moved to equalize power between these two nations, but Roosevelt made no move to create a large American presence in either Japan or China. He was nothing if not realistic about the limitations of American power or the Navy's ability to compete with the great powers that had already divided up China.

Instead, he turned his attention to his neighbors. Hegemony, after all, usually begins in the "neighborhood." Since the war cleared the Caribbean of foreign spheres, this area was the natural spot for the United States to express its newly discovered power. Groups of islands and coastal cities lent themselves to the foreign policy of a big navy. Roosevelt tackled instability through intervention and economic control, and he tackled the problem of concentrating a two-ocean navy by building the Panama Canal. The problem of passage over the isthmus and the first attempts to move a squadron from one ocean to another had bedeviled the United States since its founding years. The war with Spain exacerbated that problem, as each squadron was bound to its ocean. Enemies would not wait for ships to make the lengthy trip around the hemisphere. The effort begun before the Civil War to build a canal across the continent suddenly became a priority for President Roosevelt. The machinations involved in his effort to gain consent for an isthmian canal across Panama certainly did not constitute Roosevelt's finest hour, but the need for a canal was entirely consistent with Roosevelt's worldview of national power based upon a strong, battleship navy.

Roosevelt's Legacy

Many historians argue that the war with Spain in 1898 was the true beginning of the twentieth century. Under the leadership of Theodore Roosevelt, the first twentieth-century president, it marked the emergence of the United States as a global power. Influenced by conversations with old friends and mentors, by his experience as Assistant Secretary of the Navy, and by the causes and effects of the war with Spain, he came to office unusually well equipped for the presidency.

Roosevelt's expansionism was tied to his belief in the United States as a world power. An important component of this drive to world power was his use of the Navy to express—some would say flaunt—the power of America. He was remarkably consistent in his worldview and was clever in the use of his office to promote that view. For a president who never had to fight a war (hot or cold), he left an impressive foreign policy legacy.

On September 9, 1998, the *Washington Post* ran an advertisement sponsored by the Newport News Shipbuilding Company. The ad featured a bird's-eye view of an impressive aircraft carrier, its planes on deck in orderly rows. Above the picture of the carrier was the message: "90,000 tons of Diplomacy": Roosevelt would have approved.

Roosevelt's Management of the Navy Was Poor

James R. Reckner

Few commanders in chief were as involved in the day-to-day operations of the U.S. Navy as was Theodore Roosevelt. Partially because of his experience as assistant secretary of the navy and partially because of his own deeply held beliefs about naval power, Roosevelt was a staunch supporter of dramatic increases in the size and capability of the nation's naval forces. However, Roosevelt often involved himself too deeply in details of the Department of the Navy, at times putting himself at odds with his secretary of the navy. As a result, six different men held that post under Roosevelt. James R. Reckner contends that Roosevelt's focus on the navy was often detrimental to the functioning of the department. Reckner is a naval historian, director of the Vietnam Center at Texas Tech University, and author of *Teddy Roosevelt's Great White Fleet.*

Our Father, who art in Washington, Teddy Roosevelt be thy name. Thy will be done on the USFS Minneapolis as on all other ships. Give us this day our daily ration, consisting of sow belly, beans and hash, but deliver us from 'canned willie.'[1] Lead us from Port Royal and all other

---

1. Unhealthy, unappetizing food served to sailors by the government

Excerpted from "TR and His Navy," by James R. Reckner, *Naval History*, February 2001. Copyright © 2001 by *Naval History*. Reprinted with permission.

God-forsaken places. Make us all Special 1st Class [Lib-
ertymen] and give us all the liberty you can. Keep us
from all contagious diseases and war. Amen.

—A Sailor's Prayer

Perhaps no other president has exerted such intimate influence on the U.S. Navy as Theodore Roosevelt. The Navy was the ultimate symbol of surging American power at the beginning of the 20th century, and the
Great White Fleet's triumphant journey around the world
in 1907–1909 was as much a sign of TR's impact on the
Navy as it was of the Navy's impact on U.S. foreign policy.
His influence [was] not quite as pervasive as the prayer
above implies, though, nor were all the effects positive. In
this case, it was not Roosevelt but Upton Sinclair and his
muckraking book *The Jungle* that saved our sailors from
above canned willie. Roosevelt did initiate steps, however,
to protect enlisted men from tainted fresh meat following
the Navy's bad meat scandals during the summer of 1906.

One aspect of the Navy that never failed to command
Roosevelt's attention was pomp and ceremony. Albert
Gleaves recounts an interesting incident in his memoirs relating to ceremonies in connection with the unveiling of
the Rochambeau statue in Lafayette Square in Washington,
D.C., in May 1902. Following the unveiling, the President
and his party traveled to Annapolis, where the North Atlantic Squadron and a visiting French squadron were an-
chored. The President had lunch on board the French flag-
ship Gaulois, and on departing was offered the pageantry
of a presidential visit: all ships were fully dressed, and the
rails were manned as Roosevelt went over the side.

As the presidential yacht *Dolphin*'s handsome 14-
oared, silver-trimmed barge pulled clear of the French battleship, all ships began a 21-gun salute. Gleaves noted that
a puff of spring breeze wafted the smoke from the salute of
more than 100 guns right over the presidential barge. As

the smoke wreathed the President, Roosevelt flashed his characteristic grin, reached over and squeezed the French ambassador's knee, and said, "They say this is a relic of barbarism, but I love it!"

Love it he did, and so the Navy during the Roosevelt years participated in a wide range of naval parades and reviews, including two staged by the entire North Atlantic Fleet right in front of the President's home at Oyster Bay, Long Island, in 1903 and 1906. The Navy also played a central role in the Jamestown Tercentennial in 1907, and the famous world cruise of the Great White Fleet was the quintessential naval parade of the era. The period of TR's influence was a time of rapid and sometimes radical change in the Navy. Virtually every aspect of the Navy was affected— from the way drinking water was served to the crew to the way war plans were developed and tested. But how did the organization actually work? What influence did TR have on it? Why did he not do better by the Navy when it came to appointing Secretaries of the Navy? We still know little about what really went on in the Navy at the beginning of the 20th century, that important period of transition from an emerging modern navy to one that had "arrived."

A Passing Parade of Navy Secretaries

During the Theodore Roosevelt presidency, the affairs of the Navy were managed by six Secretaries of the Navy; they were assisted by four assistant secretaries and five Chiefs of the Bureau of Navigation. Only the General Board, with Admiral of the Navy George Dewey's steady (though uninspired) hand on the helm, provided any continuity. The remainder of the highest echelon of the naval bureaucracy was in a continuous state of flux throughout this period.

While the departure of William McKinley's secretary, John D. Long, under whom TR had served as assistant secretary in 1897 and 1898, is easily understood, the toll of the others is worth noting. Two secretaries departed unexpectedly: Paul Morton became an embarrassment and resigned when his name was linked with a rebates scandal stemming from his service as a vice president of the Atcheson, Topeka, and Santa Fe Railroad; and Victor H. Metcalf of California suffered ill health, probably from a mental breakdown. Two others—Congressman William H. Moody of Massachusetts, and lawyer Charles Jerome Bonaparte of Baltimore—agreed to assume the post with the understanding that they would hold it only temporarily, awaiting anticipated vacancies in the attorney generalship. Moody was Roosevelt's first appointment of Secretary of the Navy. From the beginning, the President treated the position like a holding pen for future appointments.

Why did TR encourage this instability at the top of the department? The most plausible answer is that he believed, as he advised Paul Morton upon his appointment, that "any honest, fairly able man" could handle the routine affairs of the department. The operational plans most concerned Roosevelt when Morton took over from Moody in 1904. In these critical matters the President believed he was better qualified to make decisions than any of his Navy secretaries. He should have been more concerned, however, about the function of the bureaucracy. As the *Army & Navy Register* commented in 1905, while each of the men appointed was "of eminent ability, it would [have been] much better for the service if a certain amount of permanency were assured in the office of secretary."

Appointments, Influence, and Other Personnel Matters

With the Assistant Secretary of the Navy, the situation was only a little less bleak. Roosevelt's first Assistant Secretary of the Navy, Frank Hackett, resigned in December 1901 to return to his private law practice. Hackett's replacement was an intimate friend of Senator Redfield Proctor of Vermont, Charles H. Darling. It was he who, according to the

Army & Navy Register, distinguished himself "when the naval establishment was threatened with the visitation of a general staff." Darling was confronted with a secretary (Moody) "who cared very little for anything which pertained to the Navy." In that situation, Darling "came forward and in an hour's testimony before the House naval committee destroyed the last lingering semblance of a general staff." Hackett also, it might be added, set the Navy's search for modernity in its organization back several years.

Claiming that he spent more money than he earned just to maintain his social position as assistant secretary, Darling sought relief and was appointed to a more lucrative customs position in Vermont. Darling's successor was Truman H. Newberry of Michigan, president of Detroit Steel and Spring Company, a naval militia officer, and veteran of the war with Spain. He relieved Victor H. Metcalf as Secretary of the Navy in the final months of the Roosevelt presidency, opening the assistant secretaryship for one final appointment, Herbert Satterlee, who was a prominent Republican, an early member of the Navy League, and the son-in-law of J. Pierpont Morgan.

One predictable result of the continual change at the top of the Navy Department was that a number of anonymous men at the middle echelon garnered considerable influence. Although the activities of these men are hard to measure, at least one incident is fairly well documented.

To gain access to the Secretary of the Navy, serving officers had to arrange an appointment through his confidential secretary, Mr. Henry Gauss, a college graduate and a man of some substance. At one point during the Bonaparte secretaryship, Deputy Paymaster General Samuel McGowan, when seeking an appointment to see the secretary, was approached by Gauss to grant an assistant paymaster commission to one of his friends. This was not unusual; most staff officer commissions were by appointment, and political connections were an important consideration when granting them. But in this case McGowan refused, because the individual already had failed his qualifying tests.

Shortly after this incident, Secretary Bonaparte received a letter from New York, laid on his desk by the same confidential secretary. In this letter the correspondent, identifying himself as a relative of McGowan, reported that the Deputy Paymaster General had told him that the commandant of the New York Navy Yard was making unauthorized use of government horses and carriages for his personal pleasure. Giving a civilian such information about a brother officer would have been a gross violation of the strict service etiquette of the day. That the report allegedly originated from a staff officer who questioned the integrity of a senior line officer would have had significant implications in the ongoing line-staff controversy. In this situation, the secretary chose to show McGowan the letter privately. McGowan, having no relatives in New York, had the letter analyzed by the Secret Service and three separate handwriting experts; the experts concluded independently that Gauss had written it. During the next several weeks a bizarre confidential correspondence passed between Bonaparte and McGowan, initially from the secretary's summer home. When Bonaparte returned to Washington, he found it necessary to travel to his law office in Baltimore to mail his letters to McGowan, whose office was in the same building as Bonaparte's in Washington. Ultimately, Bonaparte simply refused to believe that Gauss would betray his trust, and continued to employ him.

For Paymaster General H.T.B. Harris and his deputy, the seeds of distrust had been sown. When, almost concurrently with McGowan's investigation of Gauss, a scandal developed over tainted meat delivered to the New York and Norfolk Navy Yards, the paymaster general was quick to see in the unwanted publicity and the nature of the information leaked to the press the hand of Mr. Gauss once again on the attack. Harris wrote directly to Acting Secretary of the Navy Truman H. Newberry, reporting that the continuing sensation was caused by leaks to the papers by two clerks in the secretary's office. Within three days Harris had concluded that a "band of maligning conspirators" in the secretary's office was making "brazen . . . efforts" to oust him as paymaster general, and so advised President Roosevelt's personal secretary, William Loeb.

Micromanaging the Navy

A general air of distrust also existed in the Navy Department between the several bureau chiefs and between the chiefs and the secretary. Secretary John Long referred to it in his memoirs, and Secretary Bonaparte addressed it directly in a letter to the President.

In this remarkable confidential letter, also written from his law office in Baltimore to ensure confidentiality from the naval bureaucracy, Bonaparte reported that he had requested from the several bureau chiefs a detailed account of how much of a single lump-sum appropriation had been spent on each of the projects for which the money had been appropriated. The request brought replies from each of the bureaus that they could not determine what they had spent on each of the items, unless the paymaster general could furnish the data. Bonaparte also reported that this bureau could not tell how much was spent either, without going through all of the vouchers written by the Navy Department for the entire year. Bonaparte confided to Roosevelt: "I have a strong suspicion that in some of the Bureaus records are, in fact, kept from which this information could be obtained." Bonaparte concluded, however, that the chiefs involved did not "see the necessity for Congress, or even the Secretary, to know just how [they had] disposed of the money included in this lump appropriation."

Bonaparte, who considered himself a short-term secretary waiting for former Secretary Moody to vacate the attorney generalship for the Supreme Court, reported, "It undoubtedly requires a man who is interested in his work and has some force of character to keep these autonomous Bureaus in due subordination and, in fact, to retain control of the Department's work." But how could the President expect to keep a man of "some force of character" as Secretary of the Navy, when he insisted on interfering at every level and micromanaging the Navy? This micromanagement extended even to the point of personally reviewing records of midshipmen at the Naval Academy who for one reason or another were in danger of dismissal.

Roosevelt also fell into the habit of accepting correspondence directly from a few junior officers; correspondence that often suggested courses of action in direct opposition to the desires of the secretary. William S. Sims was the most famous of these correspondents; his manipulation of the President during the battleship design conference at Newport in the summer of 1908 has been well documented. But the President's support of the younger officers was at best ambivalent. At the end of the Newport Conference, for example, when the majority of the conferees sided with the bureaucrats in opposition to Sims's new battleship plans, Roosevelt went along with the majority—even though the President generally agreed with the arguments put forward by Sims and his friends. Nonetheless, the President administered a stinging rebuke to the senior officers, stating that had they been more receptive, the dreadnought battleships Utah (BB-31) and Florida (BB-30) would be "much more formidable vessels. . . . But the officials responsible for these ships seem to have limited themselves to the desire not to lag far behind other nations instead of doing what they of course ought to have done; that is, tried to lead the other nations." That, Roosevelt wrote, was not "to their credit."

In a less well-known memorandum from Sims, the then-lieutenant commander reported directly to the President (with no copy to the Secretary of the Navy) about the

Commander-in-Chief of the Atlantic Fleet's continuing poor health and his failure to carry out General Board directives to test a new battle plan, and suggested that the Commander-in-Chief, Rear Admiral Robley D. ("Fighting Bob") Evans, should be relieved. He further suggested that Rear Admiral Charles H. Davis, the second-in-command, was too near retirement to take the helm, and that the remaining admirals with the fleet, Charles M. Thomas and William H. Emory, were "in no way fitted to take up the work of training our battle fleet . . . in battle tactics."

The Naval Bureaucracy

Roosevelt, unfortunately, did not follow this bit of advice. But it was not the advice itself, but the fact that it could be given without sanction that reflects the state of the naval bureaucracy of the day. And in that respect, Roosevelt was completely responsible. "No one is to blame for this but the President, who, also, in the end is the chief sufferer," the *Army & Navy Register* reported. In this atmosphere, the senior officers in their private correspondence railed regularly against TR's "insane penchant" for "pushing young men to the front." On the other hand, the "youngsters"— themselves men in their 50s and held back for decades by a promotion system that dictated promotion solely by seniority—felt equally dissatisfied.

"My cry," wrote Commander Albert L. Key to Sims in April 1908, "is to give the 'young' officers—the misguided youths under 55—a chance, and down with the senile incompetent old grafters on the retired list, or about to retire, who must devote the whole of their time to a hopeless defense of their errors of administration while of the active list."

The bureau system, that organization of eight coequal bureaus, has been much discussed. Each had its own budget line items; each had direct control over a department in each navy yard; and, as Rear Admiral Purnell F. Harrington wrote in 1904, the bureaus "work their own sweet will in many directions, regardless of the general health of the whole machine." Each bureau chief became a rule unto himself; rarely did one leave office, revert to his original rank, and continue a normal career. Appointment to a bureau chiefship was not just a military decision; it always carried with it political connotations. Within the Navy it generally was known which politicians "controlled" the various bureau chiefs; such speculation even appears in the pages of the service journals.

The unfortunate fact is that influence was very important to the naval officers of the day. While it did not alter the glacial rate of promotion, except in appointments to bureau chiefships, it "not infrequently played a prominent role in securing for a number of officers, the detail to some desired duty." In 1902, Commander Charles S. Sperry noted, "It is melancholy but true that without some friend at court your record good or bad is waste paper. If you have friends it is equally waste paper for good or bad makes no difference."

Hurting the One You Love

Theodore Roosevelt's positive impact on the Navy is well established. The President's intimate involvement in the affairs of the Navy, however, also had two negative effects. His tendency to permit direct, unofficial correspondence from junior officers "well-nigh demoralized" those officers who did not enjoy the President's friendship [as stated by the *Army & Navy Register*]. Rear Admiral Charles M. Thomas, one of those officers on the "outside," wrote with some bitterness that Roosevelt had "six special pets in the Navy": Willard H. Brownson, Cameron McRae Winslow, Richard Wainwright, William S. Sims, Albert Gleaves, and Albert L. Key. In this respect at least, the *Army & Navy Register* editorialized, "it will be a relief to the services when Mr. Roosevelt retires to private life."

Roosevelt's close attention to the affairs of the Navy also led to most significant naval projects directly identified with the President. As an observer noted on the occasion of Paul Morton's relief of Secretary William Moody in 1904, no change in secretaries could "reverse nor long interrupt the policies favored by the President." This argument was presented as a strength of the system; but there was a less obvious negative implication.

During TR's first term his close identification with naval projects had no particularly adverse effect. In the final years of the TR presidency, however, as relations with Congress became more strained for other, non-naval reasons, the naval program was unnecessarily put at risk. In 1908, the administration engaged in a bruising battle with Congress seeking four dreadnoughts. Throughout the battle the President postponed, until too late, decisive action on reorganizing the Navy Department. Congressmen "who are not influential in initiating legislation may be very powerful in preventing it," the *Army & Navy Journal* had much earlier warned. "As a gentleman said of a watchman, who referred a prospective employer to him for a recommendation: 'He is no good as a watchman, but if you do not employ him he will set your house on fire.'"

By TR's final years in office, the need for a single strong secretary had become apparent. By then, however, Secretary Metcalf was in poor health, and one final change in office was unavoidable. Had Roosevelt been less of a micromanager (though it is not at all certain that he had it within himself to do so), and had he appointed a single strong secretary (like Josephus Daniels in the Wilson administration or John Lehman in the Reagan presidency), the Navy ultimately might have fared better. But make no mistake: it is clear that TR truly loved the Navy. It is just that in the process he unwittingly fulfilled the dictum of the old popular song, "You always hurt the one you love."

Roosevelt's Obsession with Battleships Contributed to U.S. Military Preparedness

Matthew M. Oyos

Matthew M. Oyos argues that Theodore Roosevelt not only believed in the importance of battleships, but was obsessed with the ships as a means to give the United States greater power in the world. For the president, battleships were both a manifestation of American power and a sign of the nation's ability to deploy its power around the world. During his presidency, Roosevelt campaigned vigorously for Congress to approve funds for more battleships each year, and he worked to ensure that American ships had the most sophisticated technology and armaments available. Roosevelt also worked within the Department of the Navy in order to improve ship design. For instance, he opened the design process to younger, reform-minded officers. Oyos is a professor at Radford University and has written the introductions for several reprints of Roosevelt's popular book *Rough Riders*.

AFTER WILLIAM MCKINLEY SUCCUMBED TO WOUNDS FROM an assassin's bullets in September 1901, Theodore Roosevelt brought a new generation of leadership to the

Excerpted from "Theodore Roosevelt and the Implements of War," by Matthew M. Oyos, *The Journal of Military History*, October 1996. Copyright © 1996 by *The Journal of Military History*. Reprinted with permission.

White House. The young chief executive entered office with confidence and injected fresh dynamism into the presidency. Indeed, Roosevelt was well prepared to orchestrate federal affairs, having been schooled in the rough-and-tumble world of New York state politics and having served in Washington as a Civil Service Commissioner and Assistant Secretary of the Navy. Among the many roles Roosevelt assumed as president—party leader, strike mediator, trust buster, chief diplomat, conservationist—he most eagerly embraced the duties of commander in chief. He displayed a penchant for things military throughout his life and had helped prepare the Navy for war with Spain before gaining fame in 1898 as colonel of the 1st Volunteer United States Cavalry—the Rough Riders. As president, Roosevelt sought to speed the modernization of the armed services and build forces capable of protecting the United States's new status as a great power.

Nearly a century has passed since Roosevelt became president, yet his name still evokes popular images of a hard-charging, robust leader who embodied the vibrancy of his country in the early twentieth century. His actions as commander in chief, in particular, conjure up a picture of executive assertiveness. "Walk softly and carry a big stick" remains a catch phrase for advocates of forceful diplomacy, and Roosevelt gave those words substance when he sent the Great White Fleet on a global cruise in 1907 as a display of American naval might to the rest of the world. These lingering images of a colorful, dynamic President demonstrate Roosevelt's talent for turning a phrase and for self-propagandization. They do not, however, offer a complete understanding of his actions as commander in chief. His role in this capacity is far richer and more complex than is suggested by popular perceptions of the colorful president. Although scholars have explored the intricacies of Roosevelt's political, economic, and diplomatic activities, his work as commander in chief has not received a similar amount of attention, beyond acknowledgement of his deep interest in military affairs and the use of the armed services for foreign policy ends. Roosevelt's level of involvement in military matters, in fact, varied from issue to issue, and the motivations for his actions differed as well. As a result, he did not always get what he wanted for the armed services, even if he compiled an overall record of success in his military policies.

Military Preparedness

Whatever the causes or consequences of his actions, Roosevelt was committed to improving American military preparedness. The United States had asserted itself as a great power in 1898 and signaled its intention to compete for markets and influence with the European powers and Japan. The President recognized that overseas opportunities also brought dangers, and he wanted the United States to be militarily prepared to face potential challengers. He worked to speed modernization of the armed services by raising standards for officer promotions, reforming institutions of command, building a more reliable reserve, adopting more realistic training exercises, establishing a new mission for the Marines, increasing public backing for the military services, and updating military technology. The last area, in particular, underwent considerable change in this era of industrial revolution. Militaries in the United States and other industrialized countries strained to stay abreast of the latest technological advances, and the turn of the twentieth century brought a cascade of changes: a new magazine rifle, the three-inch artillery piece, a new type of battleship, heavier-than-air flying craft, and deadlier machine guns—to name but a few. Roosevelt supported such weapons development, for he recognized that American military preparedness hinged, in part, on the ability to invent and exploit new technologies.

Roosevelt was the first president to think consistently

and coherently about the link between military technology, national military power, and foreign policy. Predecessors such as Thomas Jefferson and Abraham Lincoln had demonstrated notable interest in the tools of war, but they did not make the connection between military prowess and technology to the extent that Roosevelt did throughout his presidency. By the time Roosevelt took office, the United States was an industrial nation with overseas commitments, warfare was becoming mechanized, and Americans, like their president, held up technological advances as evidence of cultural superiority. Roosevelt's interest in these matters brought increasing demands upon his office and extended presidential activity into new realms. His efforts to promote advances in military weaponry and equipment were thus part of the development of the modern, more activist presidency. . . .

The Instruments of National Power

In contrast to his intermittent interest in airplanes and submarines, Roosevelt was nearly obsessed with battleships. These vessels represented his principal technological interest and were the focus of many inquiries and initiatives from the White House. The great ships were the core of naval power and thus were central to American security. More than any other military technology of the day, battleships lent weight to the nation's foreign policy and supported its standing as a great power. Moreover, they were prominent symbols of American industrial strength and dynamism, for the United States had lagged badly in naval technology in the 1870s and 1880s but by the early twentieth century boasted some of the most powerful vessels afloat. Roosevelt recognized the critical place of these ships in the national defense, and the importance that he placed on their design, armament, and other features underscored his belief that the commander in chief had to push continually for the most modern military technology if the United States were to remain a great power in a competitive world. To him, the President needed to keep power relationships among nations in mind at all times so that the country would not fall behind in struggles for resources, markets, and claims to political and cultural superiority. As a naval historian, he was also mindful of the tradition of building vessels that, in their class, were stouter and more heavily armed than foreign counterparts.

In keeping with this thinking, Roosevelt pushed the ongoing naval revolution to new heights in the United States. He sponsored a new type of battleship, the all-big-gun ship, which represented the greatest technological initiative of his administration apart from the building of the Panama Canal. Before 1906, battleships carried a mixed battery consisting of big guns (nine inches and above), medium-sized guns (five inches to eight inches), and smaller rapid-fire weapons for combating torpedo boats. The all-big-gun vessels would boast ten or more big guns, eliminate medium-sized ordnance, and grow in size to accommodate the larger artillery. Bigger ships theoretically meant advantages in speed, protection, and seaworthiness, and thus the all-big-gun vessels promised to outgun, outmaneuver, and outlast mixed-caliber vessels. At the time, however, the all-big-gun ship was not yet a developed and tested technology, even if rapid improvements were being made in the quality of naval gunnery. Advocates of the mixed-caliber vessel, which would close more with the enemy, claimed that it could fire much more quickly and accurately, thus negating the all-big-gun ship's advantage of a more powerful broadside fired at a greater distance. Roosevelt, in essence, had to make a decision about the likely nature of future sea battles in his choice of a battleship design.

Superiority at Sea

The idea for an all-big-gun vessel had circulated in the Navy since 1903, if not earlier, although the United States did not adopt the type until after the British launched the *Dreadnought* in 1906. The President, in fact, had begun to consider the issue of increasing size and displacement as early as 1902, after [naval strategist] Captain Alfred T. Mahan had objected to the trend of ever-larger designs and endorsed a standard type of battleship. Naval constructors, however, countered Mahan, and the White House dropped the matter. Roosevelt did not entertain the question again until 1904 after the Navy's Bureau of Construction and Repair delayed plans for an all-big-gun ship. Curious, Roosevelt asked Commander William S. Sims on 5 October 1904, if "we ought to have on our battleships merely big twelve-inch guns and fourteen-pounders, with nothing between." A maverick thinker, Sims was a relatively younger officer who had become a presidential favorite after challenging the quality of American naval gunnery early in Roosevelt's presidency. He had by-passed official channels in 1901 to present his case directly to the President. Impressed, Roosevelt put Sims in charge of improving the Navy's gunnery and frequently turned to the commander for advice. In his October 1904 inquiry, Roosevelt was interested in the implications of the all-big-gun design for naval combat power, and Sims responded immediately with a forceful argument on behalf of the new design, claiming that a ship armed with twelve eleven-inch guns could "pierce the armor of any battleship in the world at long ranges." Sims's argument no doubt resonated with the President because the commander was abreast of the latest developments in naval gunnery and because his conclusion contained the implicit message that the United States must adopt the new design or other powers would soon outclass it at sea.

Irrefutable evidence was not available in October 1904 in favor of the all-big-gun ship, and powerful voices supported the other side of the question. Captain Mahan was the most prestigious and persistent voice against the increased size of battleships. He again pushed a standard mixed-caliber type of ship as a way to reduce the pressures for naval races and to control the costs of building. Mahan's argument made little impression on Roosevelt, who was most concerned about which design would best

---

Power and Prestige

Howard K. Beale maintains that Roosevelt's drive to establish a strong navy was motivated primarily by a desire for national power and prestige.

The Roosevelt-Lodge expansionists who took the American people into an imperialist struggle for world power were not primarily concerned with American economic interests around the world. Nor did they attempt to justify expansion chiefly on economic grounds. Where they were interested in economic matters it was because economic advantages won converts to imperialist policies or enhanced the prestige of the country. Economic factors *were* important in imperialism and were to become important in American expansionist foreign policy of the twentieth century. But the primary concern of Roosevelt and his fellow-expansionists was power and prestige and the naval strength that would bring power and prestige. They gloried in the thought of American greatness and power that their expansionist policies would create. "I wish to see the United States the dominant power on the Pacific Ocean," Roosevelt wrote in 1900. "Our people are neither cravens nor weaklings and we face the future high of heart and confident of soul eager to do the great work of a great world power."

To take our place in the world we must have a great Navy, but again defense was not the chief purpose of the Navy, in spite of the fact that the big navy enthusiasts urged a larger Navy as a preserver of peace and as a defense of the country and its honor. "If we build and maintain an ade-

serve the nation's great power interests. Unless other powers followed suit, the President was not about to limit the size of American battleships and risk inferiority at sea.

The Russo-Japanese War did not settle the debate over design but, instead, added fuel to the fires of contention.

---

quate navy and let it be understood that . . . we are perfectly ready and willing to fight for our rights, then," Roosevelt believed, "the chances of war will become infinitesimal.". . . The Navy was an instrument of national policies that could not be carried out without it. "I have a horror of bluster," Roosevelt confided to John Hay, "which does not result in fight; it is both weak and undignified." He wanted us to act upon the old frontier principles, he told Lodge; "don't bluster, don't flourish your revolver and never draw unless you intend to shoot." He desired "to make all foreign powers understand that when we have adopted a line of policy we have adopted it definitely, and with the intention of backing it up with deeds as well as words."

Roosevelt, then, would have us maintain the instruments of great imperial power. We must have warships equal in numbers with "the greatness of our people." If we had a large Navy and did go to war, he urged, we would "emerge from any war immeasurably the gainer in honor and renown." He hoped this country would "take the position to which it is entitled among the nations of the earth." "If," he warned, "we announce in the beginning that we don't class ourselves among the really great peoples who are willing to fight for their greatness, that we intend to remain defenseless, . . . we doubtless can remain at peace," but "it will not be the kind of peace which tends to exalt the national name, or make the individual citizen self-respecting."

Howard K. Beale, *Theodore Roosevelt and the Rise of America to World Power*, 5th ed. Baltimore: Johns Hopkins University Press, 1966.

Admiral Togo Heihachiro dazzled observers when he dec-
imated Russia's Baltic Fleet at the Battle of Tsushima
Straits in May 1905. The victory impressed Roosevelt, and
he joined others in scrambling to learn the lessons of the
sea fight. He was curious because the outcome indicated
that medium-range guns, and not the largest guns, had in-
flicted the most damage, suggesting that the United States
might not want to adopt all-big-gun vessels too hastily.
Roosevelt turned again to Commander Sims for his views.
No all-big-gun vessels were then in service in the world,
but gunnery expert Sims projected the superiority of the
all-big-gun ship in speed, armor, and armament given the
conditions at Tsushima.

Weighing the Options

Sims's arguments swayed Roosevelt, but only for a time.
The President wanted to be absolutely certain about the
ability of all-big-gun vessels to hit the target before allocating national treasure and prestige to their construction.
These ships would be the mainstay of the Navy for years to
come, and in relying upon them Roosevelt wished neither
to risk a fatal error in military policy nor to hazard his historical reputation. For Roosevelt, the technological waters
were not yet well charted in this case, and a future conflict
might hinge on the outcome of a single sea battle. Indeed,
as [military historian] Harold Winton has written, the fog
of peace could be much denser than the fog of war as one
attempts to select the right course of action. The President
also needed to have the proper political groundwork in
place if he were to adopt a policy that would likely upset
cost-conscious and anti-imperialist members of Congress
and would contradict Captain Mahan, the most popular
prophet of the blue-water navy. Thus, Roosevelt rethought
the reliance on big guns when Mahan drew lessons from
Tsushima that favored medium guns and mixed-caliber
ships. Determined to proceed carefully, in contrast to his

public image of impetuosity, he turned to the General Board of the Navy, Sims, and Mahan in the summer of 1906 for another round of assessments before finally advocating adoption of the all-big-gun design. Sims had provided conclusive arguments in a twenty-six page letter, and Roosevelt heartily approved its publication that fall.

By then, the British had basically forced his hand with the *Dreadnought*, which they had built in one year and put to sea in October 1906. The superiority of this first all-big-gun vessel was evident to all, and its launch touched off an international race to build "dreadnoughts." Roosevelt fought immediately for the all-big-gun ship in the halls of Congress, stressing the need "to build and maintain a first-class fighting fleet" if the United States were not to "abandon every effort to keep the position which we now hold." Ironically, his deliberation in making the right choice played a part in slowing adoption of the all-big-gun type, for early calls to action from the White House would have been helpful in overcoming inertia in the Navy Department.

A Busy Chief Executive

Apart from the larger political and military considerations, Roosevelt approached the all-big-gun issue cautiously because he wanted to know as many technical details as possible before making a decision. He weighed the advantages of different gun sizes and pondered design principles concerning the weight of armor, ship displacement, sea worthiness, and other general features. His past experience as Assistant Navy Secretary doubtlessly played a role in his concern for such matters. He had become familiar with the technical aspects of battleships during his year at the Navy Department, and, because as President he acted in effect as his own Secretary of the Navy, he was going to master those details again, despite the pressures of his office. Roosevelt never acquired the expertise of a naval engineer, but for a busy chief executive his ability to digest and then repeat data and principles of ship design was astounding. His energy, appetite for reading, and mental acuity helped him to perform a variety of tasks to the amazement of contemporaries. Sims later commented that he would have difficulty imagining "any other president asking for information concerning a technical subject."

Although Roosevelt wrestled at length with the decision for the all-big-gun ship, the resolution of that issue did not end all questions of battleship design. Concerns about the quality of American battleship designs plunged him into controversy during much of 1908, a year when he would have rather concentrated on securing the election of his successor and watching the progress of the Great White Fleet on its round-the-world cruise. Reform-minded naval officers precipitated the debate in order to show that a faulty system of administration had led to dangerous deficiencies in American vessels and that a naval general staff was required to coordinate the virtually autonomous bureaus of the Navy Department. First, reformers indicted the older mixed-caliber vessels then in service with an exposé in the January 1908 issue of *McClure's Magazine*. After that effort produced no results, the naval reformers, principally Commander Sims and Commander Albert L. Key, revived the issue in spring 1908 with criticisms about the design of the battleship *North Dakota*. The *North Dakota*, still under construction, was one of America's first dreadnoughts and therefore a prototype for subsequent vessels. Key and Sims were, respectively, past and present naval aides to the President, so they presented their charges to him after the Navy Department failed to respond.

The claims of defects alarmed Roosevelt, for they threatened his battleship program, a linchpin of his foreign and military policies. The charges diminished public confidence and pride in the fleet at a time when the President wanted to retool the Navy with all-big-gun ships and had proposed four dreadnoughts in his 1907 annual message.

The allegations of defects, while intended to generate changes in the Navy's administration, could become ammunition for congressional foes of large naval budgets and expansionist foreign policies. The first charges against the older mixed-caliber ships implied that much treasure had been wasted on defective vessels, and the accusations against the *North Dakota* suggested that the new dreadnoughts were equally flawed.

After the first set of charges appeared, the President tried to reassure the public and Congress. He commissioned a series of reports on battleship design from officers representing the naval bureaus and from Commander Sims to get a reformer's opinion. Roosevelt weighed both points of view and concluded that problems existed but that the reformers "sometimes exaggerate the defects" and that "discussion is more or less academic as regards our new vessels, which are well protected in either event." His failure to support Sims, even though he had great personal regard for the man and had advanced his career, grew in part out of his distaste for the tactic of the exposé. Roosevelt, who had popularized the term "muckraker," disliked sensationalist news stories, thinking they were more destructive than constructive. In this case, muckrakers had attacked a cornerstone of United States power and prestige.

When questions surfaced about the *North Dakota*, Roosevelt decided that he needed to take stronger action. He worried in private about flaws in the new generation of battleships and confessed that he had perhaps dismissed the earlier charges too hastily: "Last year, while I became convinced that Sims, Key, . . . and the other junior officers had greatly exaggerated the defects of which they complained, I was left with the very uncomfortable feeling that there might be some real defects, and I want if possible to avoid any slip-up." The President also fretted about congressional reaction. Congress had approved two of four proposed dreadnoughts in the spring of 1908, but only after a stiff fight. Questions about the next generation of battleships would complicate Roosevelt's efforts to win approval of more vessels in the coming winter. On 24 June 1908, the President ordered Assistant Secretary of the Navy Truman Newberry to send him the plans of the *North Dakota* and to collect the views of the General Board, commanders of battleships, and younger officers with experience on battleships. Roosevelt intended to have the officers meet at the Naval War College at Newport, Rhode Island, to demonstrate that the administration sought a serious and honest review of battleship designs. If the conference found major faults with the *North Dakota*, it could at least propose remedies that would allow public and congressional faith in succeeding designs. . . .

Roosevelt delivered the opening address at Newport on 22 July 1908, and then kept a close watch on the proceedings. The conference endorsed the design of the *North Dakota*, except for a few minor changes, because construction was too advanced for major alterations. Conceding the shipbuilding bureaus a victory on the *North Dakota*, reformist and nonbureau officers sought to correct all defects on future models. . . .

A Catalyst for Innovation

Although not always getting what he wanted, Theodore Roosevelt accelerated the pace of military technological modernization despite the burdens of his office. He recognized that warfare was becoming mechanized and that a great power could not protect its interests in the world without technologically advanced armaments. During his tenure, the Navy adopted a more powerful type of battleship, the submarine gained a firmer footing in the naval arsenal, and the Army gave more serious consideration to the machine gun and the airplane. This list is not complete, but it does recount some of the projects in which Roosevelt had a hand and indicates the range and depth of his interest in technological matters.

It was the overall goal of American preparedness that motivated Roosevelt to devote so much time to military technological modernization, but other factors also informed his actions. Past military experiences were often his first frame of reference in identifying problems with the Army and offering solutions to them. In this regard, Roosevelt remained an inspired amateur who thought he had much to add to improving the military establishment even as it became more specialized and professional. Roosevelt also viewed himself as the advocate of a new generation. He used his prominent position to push the ideas of innovative, younger men before the War and Navy Department bureaucracies, which he believed were staffed by officers who were too old to grasp quickly the progress of the revolution in military technology. Roosevelt acted as a catalyst for innovation, but he was not a visionary. He was not inclined to transcend the orthodoxies of his day and push technologies such as the submarine, for example, beyond its auxiliary role. As an innovator, the President also exhibited insufficient understanding of the problems that the military faced in allocating resources and responding to competing projects. Bottlenecks in funding, skilled personnel, and supplies could present impediments to the rapid adoption of new designs and retooling of manufacturing facilities. Roosevelt was impatient for action because he felt that the United States could falter in the struggles between great nations unless it possessed military technology of the most modern type. He would have felt derelict as commander in chief if he had not fought to preserve the fighting power of the nation in this way.

In the end, Roosevelt's technological initiatives were a sign of the growing complexity of warfare and the need for the commander in chief to be aware of the capabilities of various technologies. The level of his involvement in technological questions may have been somewhat unusual, especially for a peacetime chief executive, but it pointed in the direction that presidents would have to move in the future. During the Cold War, peacetime preparedness assumed a new urgency, and a perception of presidential failure to provide for the latest military technology became a political liability at times, perhaps the most notable being the supposed "missile gap" at the end of the Eisenhower administration. Although Theodore Roosevelt did not confront the same threats in his era, he sought to avoid national humiliation by making sure that American forces possessed the best implements of war of the day.

Appendix of Documents

Document 1: Washington's Forgotten Maxim (Naval War College Address)

In his capacity as assistant secretary of the navy, on June 2, 1897, Roosevelt delivered an important address to the Naval War College in Newport, Rhode Island. In his speech he made a strong case for building a powerful navy. The speech was well received by his audience and brought Roosevelt national exposure.

A century has passed since Washington wrote "To be prepared for war is the most effectual means to promote peace." We pay to this maxim the lip loyalty we so often pay to Washington's words; but it has never sunk deep into our hearts. Indeed of late years many persons have refused it even the poor tribute of lip loyalty, and prate about the iniquity of war as if somehow that was a justification for refusing to take the steps which can alone in the long run prevent war or avert the dreadful disasters it brings in its train. The truth of the maxim is so obvious to every man of really far-sighted patriotism that its mere statement seems trite and useless; and it is not over-creditable to either our intelligence or our love of country that there should be, as there is, need to dwell upon and amplify such a truism.

In this country there is not the slightest danger of an over-development of warlike spirit, and there never has been any such danger. In all our history there has never been a time when preparedness for war was any menace to peace. On the contrary, again and again we have owed peace to the fact that we were prepared for war; and in the only contest which we have had with a European power since the Revolution, the War of 1812, the struggle and all its attendant disasters were due solely to the fact that we were not prepared to face, and were not ready instantly to resent, an attack upon our honor and interest; while the glorious triumphs at sea which redeemed that war were due to the few preparations which we had actually made. We are a great peaceful nation; a nation of merchants and manufacturers, of farmers and mechanics; a nation of workingmen, who labor incessantly with head or hand. It is idle to talk of such a nation ever being led into a course of wanton aggression or conflict with military powers by the possession of a sufficient navy.

The danger is of precisely the opposite character. If we forget that in the last resort we can only secure peace by being ready and willing to fight for it, we may some day have bitter cause to realize that a rich nation which is slothful, timid, or unwieldy is an easy prey for any people which still retains those most valuable of all qualities, the soldierly virtues. We but keep to the traditions of Washington, to the traditions of all the great Americans who struggled for the real greatness of America, when we strive to build up those fighting qualities for the lack of which in a nation, as in an individual, no refinement, no culture, no wealth, no material prosperity, can atone.

Preparation for war is the surest guaranty for peace. Arbitration is an excellent thing, but ultimately those who wish to see this country at peace with foreign nations will be wise if they place reliance upon a first-class fleet of first-class battleships rather than on any arbitration treaty which the wit of man can devise. Nelson said that the British fleet was the best negotiator in Europe, and there was much truth in the saying. Moreover, while we are sincere and earnest in our advocacy of peace, we must not forget that an ignoble peace is worse than any war. . . .

Peace is a goddess only when she comes with sword girt on thigh. The ship of state can be steered safely only when it is always possible to bring her against any foe with "her leashed thunders gathering for the leap." A really great people, proud and high-spirited, would face all the disasters of war rather than purchase that base prosperity which is bought at the price of national honor. All the great masterful races have been fighting races, and the minute that a race loses the hard fighting virtues, then, no matter what else it may retain, no matter how skilled in commerce and finance, in science or art, it has lost its proud right to stand as the equal of the best. Cowardice in a race, as in an individual, is the unpardonable sin, and a willful failure to prepare for danger may in its effects be as bad as cowardice. The timid man who cannot fight, and the selfish, short-sighted, or foolish man who will not take the steps that will enable him to fight, stand on almost the same plane.

Theodore Roosevelt, speech delivered to the National War College, Newport, Rhode Island, June 2, 1897.

Document 2: First Annual Message to Congress

In his first message to Congress, delivered in 1901, Roosevelt breaks with his predecessors and criticizes big business. Mindful of politics and the risk he was taking, he attempted to balance boldness with caution as he paved the way for the regulation of corporations.

During the last five years business confidence has been restored, and the nation is to be congratulated because of its present abounding prosperity. Such prosperity can never be created by law alone, although it is easy enough to destroy any country, if flood or drought comes, human wisdom is powerless to avert the calamity. Moreover, no law can guard us against the consequences of our own folly. The men who are idle or credulous, the men who seek gains not by genuine work with head or hand but by gambling in any form, are always a source of menace not only to themselves but to others. If the business world loses its head, it loses what legislation cannot supply. Fundamentally, the welfare of each citizen, and therefore, the welfare of the aggregate of citizens which makes the nation, must rest upon individual thrift and energy, resolution, and intelligence. Nothing can take the place of this individual capacity; but wise legislation and honest and intelligent administration can give it the fullest scope, the largest opportunity to work to good effect.

The tremendous and highly complex industrial development which went on with ever-accelerated rapidity during the latter half of the nineteenth century brings us face to face, at the beginning of the twentieth, with very serious social problems. The old laws, and the old customs which had almost the binding force of law, were once quite sufficient to regulate the accumulation and distribution of wealth. Since the industrial changes which have so enormously increased the productive power of mankind, they are no longer sufficient.

The growth of cities has gone on beyond comparison faster than the growth of the country, and the upbuilding of the great industrial centres has meant a startling increase, not merely in the aggregate of wealth, but in the number of very large individual, and especially of very large corporate, fortunes. The creation of these great corporate fortunes has not been due to the tariff nor to any other governmental action, but to natural causes in the business world, operating in other countries as they operate in our own.

The process has aroused much antagonism, a great part of which is wholly without warrant. It is not true that as the rich have grown richer the poor have grown poorer. On the contrary, never before has the average man, the wage-worker, the farmer, the small trader, been so well off as in this country and at the present time. There have been abuses connected with the accumulation of wealth; yet it remains true that a fortune accumulated in legitimate business can be accumulated by the person specially benefitted only on condition of conferring immense incidental benefits upon others. Successful enterprise, of the type which benefits all mankind, can only exist if the conditions are such as to offer great prizes as the rewards of success.

The captains of industry who have driven the railway systems across this continent, who have built up our commerce, who have developed our manufactures, have on the whole done great good to our people. Without them the material development of which we are so justly proud could never have taken place. Moreover, we should recognize the immense importance of this material development—of leaving as unhampered as is compatible with the public good the strong and forceful men upon whom the success of business operations inevitably rests. The slightest study of business conditions will satisfy anyone capable of forming a judgment that the personal equation is the most important factor in a business operation; that the business ability of the man at the head of any business concern, big or little, is usually the factor which fixes the gulf between striking success and hopeless failure.

An additional reason for caution in dealing with corporations is to be found in the international commercial conditions of to-day. The same business conditions which have produced the great aggregations of corporate and individual wealth have made them very potent factors in international commercial competition. Business concerns which have the largest means at their disposal and are managed by the ablest men are naturally those which take the lead in the strife for commercial supremacy among the nations of the world. America has only just begun to assume that commanding position in the international business world which we believe will more and more be hers. It is of the utmost importance that this position be not jeopardized, especially at a time when the over-flowing abundance of our own natural resources and the skill, business energy, and mechanical aptitude of our people make foreign markets essential. Under such conditions it would be most unwise to cramp or to fetter the youthful strength of our nation.

Moreover, it cannot too often be pointed out that to strike with ignorant violence at the interests of one set of men almost inevitably endangers the interests of all. The fundamental rule in our national life—the rule which underlies all others—is that, on the whole, and in the long run, we shall go up or down together. There are exceptions; and in times of prosperity some will prosper far more, and in times of adversity, some will suffer far more, than others; but speaking generally, a period of good times means that all share more or less in them, and in a period of hard times all feel the stress to a greater or less degree. It surely ought not to be necessary to enter into any proof of this statement; the memory of the lean years which began in 1893 is still vivid, and we can contrast them with the conditions in this very year which is now closing. Disaster to great business enterprises can never have its effects limited to the men at the top. It spreads throughout, and while it is bad for everybody, it is worst for those farthest down. The capitalist may be shorn of his luxuries; but the wage-worker may be deprived of even bare necessities.

The mechanism of modern business is so delicate that extreme care must be taken not to interfere with it in a spirit of rashness or ignorance. Many of those who have made it their vocation to denounce the great industrial combinations which are popularly, although with technical inaccuracy, known as "trusts," appeal especially to hatred and fear. These are precisely the two emotions, particularly when combined with ignorance, which unfit men for the exercise of cool and steady judgment. In facing new industrial conditions, the whole history of the world shows that legislation will generally be both unwise and ineffective unless undertaken after calm inquiry and with sober self-restraint. Much of the legislation directed at the trusts would have been exceedingly mischievous had it not also been entirely ineffective. In accordance with a well-known sociological law, the ignorant or reckless agitator has been the really effective friend of the evils which he has been nominally opposing. In dealing with business interests, for the government to undertake by crude and ill-considered legislation to do what may turn out to be bad would be to incur the risk of such far-reaching national disaster that it would be preferable to undertake nothing at all. The men who demand the impossible or the undesirable serve as the allies of the forces with which they are nominally at war, for they hamper those who would endeavor to find out in rational fashion what the wrongs really are and to what extent and in what manner it is practicable to apply remedies.

All this is true; and yet it is also true that there are real and grave evils, one of the chief being overcapitalization because of its many baleful consequences; and a resolute and practical effort must be made to correct these evils.

Theodore Roosevelt, statements from 1901 message to Congress.

Document 3: Speech at Providence

In this speech delivered in 1902, Roosevelt set the groundwork for his initiatives to regulate corporations and trusts. He praises the benefits of the country's booming economy while cautioning against the unchecked power of big business.

We are passing through a period of great commercial prosperity, and such a period is as sure as adversity itself to bring mutterings of discontent. At a time when most men prosper somewhat some men always prosper greatly; and it is as true now as when the tower of Siloam fell upon all alike, that good fortune does not come solely to the just, nor bad fortune solely to the unjust. When the weather is good for crops it is good for weeds. Moreover, not only do the wicked flourish when the times are such that most men flourish, but, what is worse, the spirit of envy and jealousy springs up in the breasts of those who, though they may be doing fairly well themselves, see others no more deserving who do better.

Wise laws and fearless and upright administration of the laws can give the opportunity for such prosperity as we see about us. But that is all that they can do. When the conditions have been created which make prosperity possible, then each individual man must achieve it for himself by his own energy and thrift and business intelligence. If when people wax fat they kick, as they have kicked since the days of Jeshurun, they will speedily destroy their own prosperity. If they go into wild speculation and lose their heads they have lost that which no laws can supply. If in a spirit of sullen envy they insist upon pulling down those who have profited most in the years of fatness, they will bury themselves in the crash of the common disaster. It is difficult to make our material condition better by the best laws, but it is easy enough to ruin it by bad laws.

The upshot of all this is that it is peculiarly incumbent upon us in a time of such material well-being, both collectively as a nation and individually as citizens, to show, each on his own account, that we possess the qualities of prudence, self-knowledge, and self-restraint. In our government we need above all things stability, fixity of economic policy; while remembering that this fixity must not be fossilization, that there must not be inability to shift our laws so as to meet our shifting national needs. There are real and great evils in our social and economic life, and these evils stand out in all their ugly baldness in time of prosperity; for the wicked who prosper are never a pleasant sight. There is every need of striving in all possible ways, individually and collectively, by combinations among ourselves and through the recognized governmental agencies, to cut out those evils. All I ask is to be sure that we do not use the knife with an ignorant zeal which would make it more dangerous to the patient than to the disease.

One of the features of the tremendous industrial development of the last generation has been the very great increase in private, and especially in corporate, fortunes. We may like this or not, just as we choose, but it is a fact nevertheless; and as far as we can see it is an inevitable result of the working of the various causes, prominent among them steam and electricity. Urban population has grown in this country, as in all civilized countries, much faster than the population as a whole during the last century. If it were not for that Rhode Island could not to-day be the State she is. Rhode Island has flourished as she has flourished because of the conditions which have brought about the great increase in urban life. There is evil in these conditions, but you can't destroy it unless you destroy the civilization they have brought about. Where men are gathered together in great masses it inevitably results that they must work far more largely through combinations than where they live scattered and remote from one another. Many of us prefer the old conditions of life, under which the average man lived more to himself and by himself, where the average community was more self-dependent, and where even though the standard of comfort was lower on the average, yet there was less of the glaring inequality in worldly conditions which we now see about us in our great cities. It is not true that the poor have grown poorer; but some of the rich have grown so very much richer that, where multitudes of men are herded together in a limited space, the contrast strikes the onlooker as more violent than formerly. On the whole, our people earn more and live better than ever before, and the progress of which we are so proud could not have taken place had it not been for the upbuilding of industrial centres, such as this in which I am speaking.

Theodore Roosevelt, August 23, 1902 speech, *Presidential Addresses and State Papers of Theodore Roosevelt,* vol. I, New York: P. F. Collier & Son, pp. 98–108.

Document 4: Meeting of the Society of American Foresters

One of Roosevelt's earliest and strongest speeches about enlightened forestry practices and the conservation of wilderness was delivered in 1903 in Washington, D.C., to the Society of American Foresters. The president shows his understanding of conservation issues in this call for the wise use of forest resources.

I have felt that this evening the meeting was of such a character as not merely to warrant but in a sense require that I should break through my custom of not coming out to make speeches of this sort. For I believe there are few bodies of men who have it in their power to do a greater service to the country than those engaged in the scientific study and practical application of improved methods of forestry for the preservation of our woods in the United States. I am glad to see here this evening not only the officials, including the head, of the Department of Agriculture, but those, like Governor Richards, most concerned in carrying out the policy of the Department of the Interior.

First and foremost, you can never afford to forget for one moment what is the object of the forest policy. Primarily that object is not to preserve forests because they are beautiful—though that is good in itself;—not to preserve them because they are refuges for the wild creatures of the wilderness—though that too is good in itself—but the primary object of the forest policy as of the land policy of the United States, is the making of prosperous homes, is part of the traditional policy of home-making of our country. Every other consideration comes as secondary. The whole effort of the government in dealing with the forests must be directed to this end, keeping in view the fact that it is not only necessary to start the homes as prosperous, but to keep them so. That is the way the forests have need to be kept. You can start a prosperous home by destroying the forest, but you do not keep it. You will be able to make that policy permanently the policy of the country only in so far as you are able to make the people at large, and then all the people concretely, interested in the results in the different localities, appreciative of what it means; give them a full recognition of its value, and make them earnest and zealous adherents of it. Keep that in mind too. In a government such as ours it is out of the question to impose a policy like this upon the people from without. A permanent policy can come only from the intelligent conviction of the people themselves that it is wise, and useful; nay, indispensable. We shall decide in the long run whether we will or will not preserve the forests of the Rocky Mountains accordingly as we are or are not able to make the people of the States around the mountains, in their neighborhood, hearty believers in the policy of forest preservation. This is the only way in which this policy can be made a permanent success. In other words, you must convince the people of the truth—and it is the truth—that the success of home-makers depends in the long run upon the wisdom with which the Nation takes care of its forests. That seems a strong statement. It is none too strong. There are small sections of this country where what is done with the woodlands makes no difference; but over the great extent of the country the ultimate well-being of the home-maker will depend in very large part upon the intelligent use made of the forests. In other words, you, yourselves, must keep this practical object before your mind. You must remember that the forest which contributes nothing to the wealth, progress, or safety of the country is of no interest to the government, and it should be of little to the forester. Your attention should be directed not to the preservation of the forests as an end in itself, but as the means for preserving and increasing the prosperity of the Nation. Forestry is the preservation of forests by wise use. We shall succeed, not by preventing the use, but by making the forests of use to the settler, the rancher, the miner, the man who lives in the neighborhood, and indirectly the man who may live hundreds of miles off, down the course of some great river which has its rise among the forests.

Theodore Roosevelt, statements from March 26, 1903.

Document 5: Speech at Yellowstone National Park

During a ceremony in 1903 to lay the first stone of what would become the entrance to Yellowstone, Roosevelt spoke on the beauty and importance of the park and encouraged citizens to visit, enjoy, and protect it. He asserted his belief in conservation and in so doing became the first president to articulate such commitment to natural resources.

It is a pleasure now to say a few words to you at the laying of the cornerstone of the beautiful road which is to mark the entrance to this park. The Yellowstone Park is something absolutely unique in the world, so far as I know. Nowhere else in any civilized country is there to be found such a tract of veritable wonderland made accessible to all visitors, where at the same time not only the scenery of the wilderness but the wild creatures of the park are scrupulously preserved; the only change being that these same wild creatures have been so carefully protected as to show a literally astounding tameness. The creation and preservation of such a great natural playground in the interest of our people as a whole is a credit to the nation; but above all a credit to Montana, Wyoming, and Idaho. It has been preserved with wise foresight. The scheme of its preservation is noteworthy in its essential democracy. Private game preserves, though they may be handled in such a way as to be not only good things for themselves, but good things for the surrounding community, can yet never be more than poor substitutes, from the standpoint of the public, for great national playgrounds such as this Yellowstone Park. This park was created, and is now administered, for the benefit and enjoyment of the people. The government must continue to appropriate for it especially in the direction of completing and perfecting an excellent system of driveways. But already its beauties can be seen with great comfort in a short space of time and at an astoundingly small cost, and with the sense on the part of every visitor that it is in part his property, that it is the property of Uncle Sam and therefore of all of us. The only way that the people as a whole can secure to themselves and their children the enjoyment in perpetuity of what the Yellowstone Park has to give is by assuming the ownership in the name of the nation and by jealously safeguarding and preserving the scenery, the forests, and the wild creatures. When we have a good system of carriage roads throughout the park—for of course it would be very unwise to allow either steam or electric roads in the park—we shall have a region as easy and accessible to travel in as it is already every whit as interesting as any similar territory of the Alps or the Italian Riviera. The geysers, the extraordinary hot springs, the lakes, the mountains, the canyons, and cataracts unite to make this region something not wholly to be paralleled elsewhere on the globe. It must be kept for the benefit and enjoyment of all of us; and I hope to see a steadily increasing number of our people take advantage of its attractions. At present it is rather singular that a greater number of people come from Europe to see it than come from our own eastern states. The people nearby seem awake to its beauties; and I hope that more and more of our people who dwell far off will appreciate its really marvelous character. Incidentally, I should like to point out that some time people will surely awake to the fact that the park has special beauties to be seen in winter; and any hardy man who can go through it in that season on skis will enjoy himself as he scarcely could elsewhere. . . .

The preservation of the forests is of course the matter of prime importance in every public reserve of this character. In this region of the Rocky Mountains and the Great Plains the problem of the water supply is the most important which the home-maker has to face. Congress has not of recent years done anything wiser than in passing the irrigation bill; and nothing is more essential to the preservation of the water supply than the preservation of the forests. Montana has in its water power a source of development which has hardly yet been touched. This water power will be seriously impaired if ample protection is not given the forests. Therefore this park, like the forest reserves generally, is of the utmost advantage to the country around from the merely utilitarian side. But of course this park, also because of its peculiar features, is to be preserved as a beautiful natural playground. Here all the wild creatures of the old days are being preserved, and their overflow into the surrounding country means that the people of the surrounding country, so long as they see that the laws are observed by all, will be able to ensure to themselves and to their children and to their children's children much of the old-time pleasure of the hardy life of the wilderness and of the hunter in the wilderness. This pleasure, moreover, can under such conditions be kept for all who have the love of adventure and the hardihood to take advantage of it, with small regard for what their fortune may be. I cannot too often repeat that the essential feature in the present management of the Yellowstone Park, as in all similar places, is its essential democracy—it is the preservation of the scenery, of the forests, of the wilderness life and the wilderness game for the people as a whole, instead of leaving the enjoyment thereof to be confined to the very rich who can control private reserves. I have been literally astounded at the enormous quantities of elk and at the number of deer, antelope, and mountain sheep which I have seen on their wintering grounds; and the deer and sheep in particular are quite as tame as range stock. A few buffalo are being preserved. I wish very much that the government could somewhere provide for an experimental breeding station of crossbreeds between buffalo and the common cattle. If these crossbreeds could be successfully perpetuated we should have animals which would produce a robe quite as good as the old buffalo robe with which twenty years ago everyone was familiar, and animals moreover which would be so hardy that I think they would have a distinct commercial importance. They would, for instance, be admirably suited for Alaska, a territory which I look to see develop astoundingly within the next decade or two, not only because of its furs and fisheries, but because of its agricultural and pastoral possibilities.

Theodore Roosevelt, statements from April 24, 1903.

Document 6: Message to Congress on the Panama Canal

The Congress and the nation were divided on the politically charged issue of building a canal across Panama to provide an accessible waterway between the Atlantic and Pacific Oceans. Nicaragua had been proposed as an alternative site for the canal, the relations with Colombia (who governed Panama) were strained, and concerns about high costs and whether or not the project would succeed loomed as Roosevelt boldly set forth his plan and answered critics in this 1904 speech.

To the Senate and House of Representatives: I lay before the Congress for its information a statement of my action up to this time in executing the act entitled "An Act to Provide for the Construction of a Canal Connecting the Waters of the Atlantic and Pacific Oceans," approved June 28, 1902.

By the said act the president was authorized to secure for the United States the property of the Panama Canal Company and the perpetual control of a strip six miles wide across the Isthmus of Panama. It was further provided that "should the president be unable to obtain for the United States a satisfactory title to the property of the New Panama Canal Company and the control of the necessary territory of the Republic of Colombia . . . within a reasonable time and upon reasonable terms, then the president" should endeavor to provide for a canal by the Nicaragua route. The language quoted defines with exactness and precision what was to be done, and what as a matter of fact has been done. The president was authorized to go to the Nicaragua route only if within a reasonable time he could not obtain "control of the necessary territory of the Republic of Colombia." This control has now been obtained; the provision of the act has been complied with; it is no longer possible under existing legislation to go to the Nicaragua route as an alternative.

This act marked the climax of the effort on the part of the United States to secure, so far as legislation was concerned, an interoceanic canal across the Isthmus. The effort to secure a treaty for this purpose with one of the Central American republics did not stand on the same footing with the effort to secure a treaty under any ordinary conditions. The proper position for the United States to assume in reference to this canal, and therefore to the governments of the Isthmus, had been clearly set forth by Secretary Cass in 1858. . . .

The United States has taken the position that no other government is to build the canal. In 1889, when France proposed to come to the aid of the French Panama Company by guaranteeing their bonds, the Senate of the United States in executive session, with only some three votes dissenting, passed a resolution as follows:

> That the government of the United States will look with serious concern and disapproval upon any connection of any European government with the construction or control of any ship canal across the Isthmus of Darien or across Central America, and must regard any such connection or control as injurious to the just rights and interests of the United States and as a menace to their welfare.

Under the Hay-Pauncefote Treaty it was explicitly provided that the United States should control, police, and protect the canal which was to be built, keeping it open for the vessels of all nations on equal terms. The United States thus assumed the position of guarantor of the canal and of its peaceful use by all the world. The guarantee included as a matter of course the building of the canal. The enterprise was recognized as responding to an international need; and it would be the veriest travesty on right and justice to treat the governments in possession of the Isthmus as having the right, in the language of Mr. Cass, "to close the gates of intercourse on the great highways of the world, and justify the act by the pretension that these avenues of trade and travel belong to them and that they choose to shut them."

When this government submitted to Colombia the Hay-Herran Treaty three things were, therefore, already settled.

One was that the canal should be built. The time for delay, the time for permitting the attempt to be made by private enterprise, the time for permitting any government of antisocial spirit and of imperfect development to bar the work was past. The United States had assumed in connection with the canal certain responsibilities not only to its own people, but to the civilized world, which imperatively demanded that there should no longer be delay in beginning the work.

Second. While it was settled that the canal should be built without unnecessary or improper delay, it was no less clearly shown to be our purpose to deal not merely in a spirit of justice but in a spirit of generosity with the people through whose land we might build it. The Hay-Herran Treaty, if it erred at all, erred in the direction of an overgenerosity toward the Colombian government. In our anxiety to be fair we had gone to the very verge in yielding to a weak nation's demands what that nation was helplessly unable to enforce from us against our will. The only criticisms made upon the administration for the terms of the Hay-Herran Treaty were for having granted too much to Colombia, not for failure to grant enough. Neither in the Congress nor in the public press, at the time that this treaty was formulated, was there complaint that it did not in the fullest and amplest manner guarantee to Colombia everything that she could by any color of title demand.

Nor is the fact to be lost sight of that the rejected treaty, while generously responding to the pecuniary demands of Colombia, in other respects merely provided for the construction of the canal in conformity with the express requirements of the act of the Congress of June 28, 1902. By that act, as heretofore quoted, the president was authorized to acquire from Colombia, for the purposes of the canal, "perpetual control" of a certain strip of land; and it was expressly required that the "control" thus to be obtained should include "jurisdiction" to make police and sanitary regulations and to establish such judicial tribunals as might be agreed on for their enforcement. These were conditions precedent prescribed by the Congress; and for their fulfillment suitable stipulations were embodied in the treaty. . . . During all the years of negotiation and discussion that preceded the conclusion of the Hay-Herran Treaty, Colombia never intimated that the requirement by the United States of control over the canal strip would render unattainable the construction of a canal by way of the Isthmus of Panama; nor were we advised, during the months when legislation of 1902 was pending before the Congress, that the terms which it embodied would render negotiations with Colombia impracticable. It is plain that no nation could construct and guarantee the neutrality of the canal with a less degree of control than was stipulated for in the Hay-Herran Treaty. A refusal to grant such degree of control was necessarily a refusal to make any practicable treaty at all. Such refusal therefore squarely raised the question whether Colombia was entitled to bar the transit of the world's traffic across the Isthmus.

That the canal itself was eagerly demanded by the people of the locality through which it was to pass, and that the people of this locality no less eagerly longed for its construction under American control, are shown by the unanimity of action in the new Panama Republic. Furthermore, Colombia, after having rejected the treaty in spite of our protests and warnings when it was in her power to accept it, has since shown the utmost eagerness to accept the same treaty if only the status quo could be restored. One of the men standing highest in the official circles of Colombia, on November 6, addressed the American minister at Bogota, saying that if the government of the United States would land troops to preserve Colombian sovereignty and the transit, the Colombian government would "declare martial law; and, by virtue of vested constitutional authority, when public order is disturbed, [would] approve by decree the ratification of the canal treaty as signed; or, if the government of the United States prefers, [would] call extra session of the Congress—with new and friendly members—next May to approve the treaty." Having these facts in view, there is no shadow of question that the government of the United States proposed a treaty which was not merely just, but generous to Colombia, which our people regarded as erring, if at all, on the side of overgenerosity; which was hailed with delight by the people of the immediate locality through which the canal was to pass, who were most concerned as to the new order of things; and which the Colombia authorities now recognize as being so good that they are willing to promise its unconditional ratification if only we will desert those who have shown themselves our friends and restore to those who have shown themselves unfriendly the power to undo what they did. . . .

Third. Finally the Congress definitely settled where the canal was to be built. It was provided that a treaty should be made for building the canal across the Isthmus of Panama; and if, after reasonable time, it proved impossible to secure such treaty, that then we should go to Nicaragua. The treaty has been made; for it needs no argument to show that the intent of the Congress was to ensure a canal across Panama, and that whether the republic granting the title was called New Granada, Colombia, or Panama mattered not one whit. As events turned out, the question of "reasonable time" did not enter into the matter at all. Although, as the months went by, it became increasingly improbable that the Colombian Congress would ratify the treaty or take steps which would be equivalent thereto, yet all chance for such action on their part did not vanish until the Congress closed at the end of October; and within three days thereafter the revolution in Panama had broken out. Panama became an independent state, and the control of the territory necessary for building the canal then became obtainable. The condition under which alone we could have gone to Nicaragua thereby became impossible of fulfillment. If the pending treaty with Panama should not be ratified by the Senate this would not alter the fact that we could not go to Nicaragua. The Congress has decided the route, and there is no alternative under existing legislation.

Theodore Roosevelt, statements from January 4, 1904.

Document 7: Inaugural Address

Because Roosevelt had ascended to the presidency on the death of William McKinley in 1901, his 1905 inaugural address was his first. In grand terms, Roosevelt appealed for support of what he deemed to be the nation's new and vital rise to greatness.

My Fellow Citizens: No people on earth have more cause to be thankful than ours, and this is said reverently, in no spirit of boastfulness in our own strength, but with gratitude to the Giver of Good, who has blessed us with the conditions which have enabled us to achieve so large a measure of well-being and of happiness. To us as a people it has been granted to lay the foundations of our national life in a new continent. We are the heirs of the ages, and yet we have had to pay few of the penalties which in old countries are exacted by the dead hand of a bygone civilization. We have not been obliged to fight for our existence against any alien race; and yet our life has called for the vigor and effort without which the manlier and hardier virtues wither away. Under such conditions it would be our own fault if we failed; and the success which we have had in the past, the success which we confidently believe the future will bring, should cause in us no feeling of vainglory, but rather a deep and abiding realization of all which life has offered us; a full acknowledgment of the responsibility which is ours; and a fixed determination to show that under a free government a mighty people can thrive best, alike as regards the things of the body and the things of the soul.

Much has been given to us, and much will rightfully be expected from us. We have duties to others and duties to ourselves; and we can shirk neither. We have become a great nation, forced by the fact of its greatness into relations with the other nations of the earth; and we must behave as beseems a people with such responsibilities. Toward all other nations, large and small, our attitude must be one of cordial and sincere friendship. We must show not only in our words but in our deeds that we are earnestly desirous of securing their goodwill by acting toward them in a spirit of just and generous recognition of all their rights. But justice and generosity in a nation, as in an individual, count most when shown not by the weak but by the strong. While ever careful to refrain from wronging others, we must be no less insistent that we are not wronged ourselves. We wish peace; but we wish the peace of justice, the peace of righteousness. We wish it because we think it is right and not because we are afraid. No weak nation that acts manfully and justly should ever have cause to fear us, and no strong power should ever be able to single us out as a subject for insolent aggression.

Our relations with the other powers of the world are important; but still more important are our relations among ourselves. Such growth in wealth, in population, and in power as this nation has seen during the century and a quarter of its national life is inevitably accompanied by a like growth in the problems which are ever before every nation that rises to greatness. Power invariably means both responsibility and danger. Our forefathers faced certain perils which we have outgrown. We now face other perils the very existence of which it was impossible that they should foresee. Modern life is both complex and intense, and the tremendous changes wrought by the extraordinary industrial development of the last half century are felt in every fiber of our social and political being. Never before have men tried so vast and formidable an experiment as that of administering the affairs of a continent under the forms of a democratic republic. The conditions which have told for our marvelous material well-being, which have developed to a very high degree our energy, self-reliance, and individual initiative, have also brought the care and anxiety inseparable from the accumulation of great wealth in industrial centers. Upon the success of our experiment much depends; not only as regards our own welfare, but as regards the welfare of mankind. If we fail, the cause of free self-government throughout the world will rock to its foundations; and therefore our responsibility is heavy, to ourselves, to the world as it is today, and to the generations yet unborn. There is no good reason why we should fear the future, but there is every reason why we should face it seriously, neither hiding from ourselves the gravity of the problems before us nor fearing to approach these problems with the unbending, unflinching purpose to solve them aright.

Yet, after all, though the problems are new, though the tasks set before us differ from the tasks set before our fathers who founded and preserved this Republic, the spirit in which these tasks must be undertaken and these problems faced, if our duty is to be well done, remains essentially unchanged. We know that self-government is difficult. We know that no people needs such high traits of character as that people which seeks to govern its affairs aright through the freely expressed will of the freemen who compose it. But we have faith that we shall not prove false to the memories of the men of the mighty past. They did their work; they left us the splendid heritage we now enjoy. We in our turn have an assured confidence that we shall be able to leave this heritage unwasted and enlarged to our children and our children's children. To do so we must show, not merely in great crises, but in the everyday affairs of life, the qualities of practical intelligence, of courage, of hardihood and endurance, and above all the power of devotion to a lofty ideal, which made great the men who founded this Republic in the days of Washington, which made great the men who preserved this Republic in the days of Abraham Lincoln.

Theodore Roosevelt, inaugural address, March 4, 1905.

Document 8: Eighth Annual Message to Congress

At the end of his presidency, Roosevelt was a much more confident and commanding figure than he was in 1901. In this 1908 message to Congress, he called for expanding the powers of the Interstate Commerce Commission and warned of the dangers of unrestricted corporate power.

As regards the great corporations engaged in interstate business, and especially the railroad, I can only repeat what I have already again and again said in my messages to the Congress. I believe that under the interstate clause of the Constitution the United States has complete and paramount right to control all agencies of interstate commerce; and I believe that the National Government alone can exercise this right with wisdom and effectiveness so as both to secure justice from, and to do justice to, the great corporations which are the most important factors in modern business. I believe that it is worse than folly to attempt to prohibit all combinations as is done by the Sherman antitrust law, because such a law can be enforced only imperfectly and unequally, and its enforcement works almost as much hardship as good. I strongly advocate that instead of an unwise effort to prohibit all combinations there shall be substituted a law which shall expressly permit combinations which are in the interest of the public, but shall at the same time give to some agency of the National Government full power of control and supervision over them. One of the chief features of this control should be securing entire publicity in all matters which the public has a right to know, and furthermore, the power, not by judicial but by executive action, to prevent or put a stop to every form of improper favoritism or other wrong-doing.

The railways of the country should be put completely under the Interstate Commerce Commission and removed from the domain of the antitrust law. The power of the commission should be made thoroughgoing, so that it could exercise complete supervision and control over the issue of securities as well as over the raising and lowering of rates. As regards rates, at least, this power should be summary. The power to investigate the financial operations and accounts of the railways has been one of the most valuable features in recent legislation. Power to make combinations and traffic agreements should be explicitly conferred upon the railroads, the permission of the commission being first gained and the combination or agreement being published in all its details. In the interest of the public the representatives of the public should have complete power to see that the railroads do their duty by the public, and as a matter of course this power should also be exercised so as to see that no injustice is done to the railroads. The shareholders, the employees, and the shippers all have interests that must be guarded. It is to the interest of all of them that no swindling stock speculation should be allowed, and that there should be no improper issuance of securities. The guiding intelligences necessary for the successful building and successful management of railroads should receive ample remuneration; but no man should be allowed to make money in connection with railroads out of fraudulent overcapitalization and kindred stock-gambling performances; there must be no defrauding of investors, oppression of the farmers and business men who ship freight, or callous disregard of the rights and needs of the employees. In addition to this the interests of the shareholders, of the employees, and of the shippers should all be guarded as against one another. To give any one of them undue and improper consideration is to do injustice to the others. Rates must be made as low as is compatible with giving proper returns to all the employees of the railroad, from the highest to the lowest, and proper returns to the shareholders; but they must not, for instance, be reduced in such fashion as to necessitate a cut in the wages of the employees or the abolition of the proper and legitimate profits of honest shareholders.

Telegraph and telephone companies engaged in interstate business should be put under the jurisdiction of the Interstate Commerce Commission.

It is very earnestly to be wished that our people, through their representatives, should act in this matter. It is hard to say whether most damage to the country at large would come from entire failure on the part of the public to supervise and control the actions of the great corporations, or from the exercise of the necessary governmental power in a way which would do injustice and wrong to the corporations. Both the preachers of an unrestricted individualism, and the preachers of an oppression which would deny to able men of business the just reward of their initiative and business sagacity, are advocating policies that would be fraught with the gravest harm to the whole country. To permit every lawless capitalist, every law-defying corporation, to take any action, no matter how iniquitous, in the effort to secure an improper profit and to build up privilege, would be ruinous to the Republic and would mark the abandonment of the effort to secure in the industrial world the spirit of democratic fair dealing. On the other hand, to attack these wrongs in that spirit of demagogy which can see wrong only when committed by the man of wealth, and is dumb and blind in the presence of wrong committed against men of property or by men of no property, is exactly as evil as corruptly to defend the wrong-doing of men of wealth. The war we wage must be waged against misconduct, against wrong-doing wherever it is found; and we must stand heartily for the rights of every decent man, whether he be a man of great wealth or a man who earns his livelihood as a wage-worker or a tiller of the soil.

Theodore Roosevelt, statements from 1908 message to Congress.

Document 9: Speech Before the Conference on the Conservation of Natural Resources

As president, Roosevelt convened important conferences on conservation issues. At an event held at the White House in 1908, he impresses upon

*the governors of the states the importance of conserving natural re-
sources, an issue he boldly proclaims to be "the weightiest problem now
before the nation."*

Governors of the Several States, and Gentlemen: I welcome you to this
conference at the White House. You have come hither at my request so
that we may join together to consider the question of the conservation
and use of the great fundamental sources of wealth of this nation. So
vital is this question that for the first time in our history the chief executive officers of the states separately, and of the state together forming the nation, have met to consider it.

With the governors come men from each state chosen for their special acquaintance with the terms of the problem that is before us.
Among them are experts in natural resources and representatives of
national organizations concerned in the development and use of these
resources; the senators and representatives in Congress; the Supreme
Court, the Cabinet, and the Inland Waterways Commission have likewise been invited to the conference, which is therefore national in a peculiar sense.

This conference on the conservation of natural resources is in effect
a meeting of the representatives of all the people of the United States
called to consider the weightiest problem now before the nation; and
the occasion for the meeting lies in the fact that the natural resources
of our country are in danger of exhaustion if we permit the old wasteful methods of exploiting them longer to continue.

With the rise of peoples from savagery to civilization, and with the
consequent growth in the extent and variety of the needs of the average man, there comes a steadily increasing growth of the amount demanded by this average man from the actual resources of the country.
Yet, rather curiously, at the same time the average man is apt to lose his
realization of this dependence upon nature.

Savages, and very primitive peoples generally, concern themselves
only with superficial natural resources; with those which they obtain
from the actual surface of the ground. As peoples become a little less
primitive, their industries, although in a rude manner, are extended to
resources below the surface; then, with what we call civilization and
the extension of knowledge, more resources come into use, industries
are multiplied, and foresight begins to become a necessary and prominent factor in life. Crops are cultivated; animals are domesticated; and
metals are mastered.

Every step of the progress of mankind is marked by the discovery
and use of natural resources previously unused. Without such pro-

gressive knowledge and utilization of natural resources population could not grow, nor industries multiply, nor the hidden wealth of the earth be developed for the benefit of mankind.

From the first beginnings of civilization, on the banks of the Nile and the Euphrates, the industrial progress of the world has gone on slowly, with occasional setbacks, but on the whole steadily, through tens of centuries to the present day. But of late the rapidity of the process has increased at such a rate that more space has been actually covered during the century and a quarter occupied by our national life than during the preceding six thousand years that take us back to the earliest monuments of Egypt, to the earliest cities of the Babylonian plain.

When the founders of this nation met at Independence Hall in Philadelphia the conditions of commerce had not fundamentally changed from what they were when the Phoenician keels first furrowed the lonely waters of the Mediterranean. The differences were those of degree, not of kind, and they were not in all cases even those of degree. Mining was carried on fundamentally as it had been carried on by the pharaohs in the countries adjacent to the Red Sea.

The wares of the merchants of Boston, of Charleston, like the wares of the merchants of Nineveh and Sidon, if they went by water, were carried by boats propelled by sails or oars; if they went by land they were carried in wagons drawn by beasts of draft or in packs on the backs of beasts of burden. The ships that crossed the high seas were better than the ships that had once crossed the Aegean, but they were of the same type, after all—they were wooden ships propelled by sails; and on land, the roads were not as good as the roads of the Roman Empire, while the service of the posts was probably inferior.

In Washington's time anthracite coal was known only as a useless black stone; and the great fields of bituminous coal were undiscovered. As steam was unknown, the use of coal for power production was undreamed of. Water was practically the only source of power, save the labor of men and animals; and this power was used only in the most primitive fashion. But a few small iron deposits had been found in this country, and the use of iron by our countrymen was very small. Wood was practically the only fuel, and what lumber was sawed was consumed locally, while the forests were regarded chiefly as obstructions to settlement and cultivation.

Such was the degree of progress to which civilized mankind had attained when this nation began its career. It is almost impossible for us in this day to realize how little our Revolutionary ancestors knew of the great store of natural resources whose discovery and use have been such vital factors in the growth and greatness of this nation, and how little they required to take from this store in order to satisfy their needs.

Since then our knowledge and use of the resources of the present territory of the United States have increased a hundred-fold. Indeed, the growth of this nation by leaps and bounds makes one of the most striking and important chapters in the history of the world. Its growth has been due to the rapid development, and alas! that it should be said, to the rapid destruction of our natural resources. Nature has supplied to us in the United States, and still supplies to us, more kinds of resources in a more lavish degree than has ever been the case at any other time or with any other people. Our position in the world has been attained by the extent and thoroughness of the control we have achieved over nature; but we are more, and not less, dependent upon what she furnishes than at any previous time of history since the days of primitive man.

Yet our fathers, though they knew so little of the resources of the country, exercised a wise forethought in reference thereto. Washington clearly saw that the perpetuity of the states could only be secured by union, and that the only feasible basis of union was an economic one; in other words, that it must be based on the development and use of their natural resources. Accordingly, he helped to outline a scheme of commercial development, and by his influence an interstate waterways commission was appointed by Virginia and Maryland.

It met near where we are now meeting, in Alexandria, adjourned to Mount Vernon, and took up the consideration of interstate commerce by the only means then available, that of water. Further conferences were arranged, first at Annapolis, and then at Philadelphia. It was in Philadelphia that the representatives of all the states met for what was in its original conception merely a waterways conference; but when they had closed their deliberations the outcome was the Constitution which made the states into a nation.

The Constitution of the United States thus grew in large part out of the necessity for united action in the wise use of one of our natural resources. The wise use of all of our natural resources, which are our national resources as well, is the great material question of today. I have asked you to come together now because the enormous consumption of these resources, and the threat of imminent exhaustion of some of them, due to reckless and wasteful use, once more calls for common effort, common action.

Theodore Roosevelt, statements from May 13, 1908.

Document 10: Speech at Milwaukee, Wisconsin

Roosevelt came out of retirement in 1912 to again seek the presidency, initially as a Republican challenger to incumbent president Howard Taft and later as the nominee of the Progressive Party. While campaigning in Wisconsin the president was shot in the chest but survived and delivered this remarkable speech.

Friends, I shall ask you to be as quiet as possible. I don't know whether you fully understand that I have just been shot; but it takes more than that to kill a bull moose. But fortunately I had my manuscript, so you see I was going to make a long speech, and there is a bullet—there is where the bullet went through—and it probably saved me from it going into my heart. The bullet is in me now, so that I cannot make a very long speech, but I will try my best.

And now, friends, I want to take advantage of this incident and say a word of solemn warning to my fellow countrymen. First of all, I want to say this about myself: I have altogether too important things to think of to feel any concern over my own death; and now I cannot speak to you insincerely within five minutes of being shot. I am telling you the literal truth when I say that my concern is for many other things. It is not in the least for my own life. I want you to understand that I am ahead of the game, anyway. No man has had a happier life than I have led; a happier life in every way. I have been able to do certain things that I greatly wished to do, and I am interested in doing other things. I can tell you with absolute truthfulness that I am very much uninterested in whether I am shot or not. It was just as when I was colonel of my regiment. I always felt that a private was to be excused for feeling at times some pangs of anxiety about his personal safety, but I cannot understand a man fit to be a colonel who can pay any heed to his personal safety when he is occupied as he ought to be occupied with the absorbing desire to do his duty.

I am in this cause with my whole heart and soul. I believe that the Progressive movement is for making life a little easier for all our people; a movement to try to take the burdens off the men and especially the women and children of this country. I am absorbed in the success of that movement.

Friends, I ask you now this evening to accept what I am saying as absolutely true, when I tell you I am not thinking of my own success. I am not thinking of my life or of anything connected with me personally. I am thinking of the movement. I say this by way of introduction, because I want to say something very serious to our people and especially to the newspapers. I don't know anything about who the man was who shot me tonight. He was seized at once by one of the stenographers in my party, Mr. Martin, and I suppose is now in the hands of the police. He shot to kill. He shot—the shot, the bullet went in here—I will show you.

I am going to ask you to be as quiet as possible for I am not able to give the challenge of the bull moose quite as loudly. Now, I do not know who he was or what party he represented. He was a coward. He stood in the darkness in the crowd around the automobile and when they cheered me, and I got up to bow, he stepped forward and shot me in the darkness.

Now, friends, of course, I do not know, as I say, anything about him; but it is a very natural thing that weak and vicious minds should be inflamed to acts of violence by the kind of awful mendacity and abuse that have been heaped upon me for the last three months by the papers in the interest of not only Mr. Debs but of Mr. Wilson and Mr. Taft.

Friends, I will disown and repudiate any man of my party who attacks with such foul slander and abuse any opponent of any other party; and now I wish to say seriously to all the daily newspapers, to the Republican, the Democratic, and the Socialist parties, that they cannot, month in and month out and year in and year out, make the kind of untruthful, of bitter assault that they have made and not expect that brutal, violent natures, or brutal and violent characters—especially when the brutality is accompanied by a not very strong mind—they cannot expect that such natures will be unaffected by it.

Now, friends, I am not speaking for myself at all. I give you my word, I do not care a rap about being shot; not a rap.

Theodore Roosevelt, statements from October 14, 1912.

Document 11: America the Unready

Roosevelt continued to wield influence in retirement. In his autobiography, published in 1913, he comments on the importance of the nation's continual preparedness for war.

I suppose the United States will always be unready for war, and in consequence will always be exposed to great expense, and to the possibility of the gravest calamity, when the nation goes to war. This is no new thing. Americans learn only from catastrophes and not from experience.

There would have been no war in 1812 if, in the previous decade, America, instead of announcing that "peace was her passion," instead of acting on the theory that unpreparedness averts war, had been willing to go to the expense of providing a fleet of a score of ships of the line. However, in that case, doubtless the very men who in the actual event deplored the loss of life and waste of capital which their own supineness had brought about would have loudly inveighed against the "excessive and improper cost of armaments"; so it all came to about the same thing in the end.

There is no more thoroughgoing international Mrs. Gummidge, and no more utterly useless and often utterly mischievous citizen, than the peace-at-any-price, universal-arbitration type of being, who is always complaining either about war or else about the cost of the armaments which act as the insurance against war. There is every reason why we should try to limit the cost of armaments, as these tend to grow excessive, but there is also every reason to remember that in the present stage of civilization a proper armament is the surest guaranty of peace—and is the only guaranty that war, if it does come, will not mean irreparable and overwhelming disaster. In the spring of 1897 President McKinley appointed me assistant secretary of the navy. I owed the appointment chiefly to the efforts of Senator H.C. Lodge, of Massachusetts, who doubtless was actuated mainly by his long and close friendship for me, but also—I like to believe—by his keen interest in the navy. The first book I had ever published, fifteen years previously, was *The History of the Naval War of 1812*; and I have always taken the interest in the navy which every good American ought to take. At the time I wrote the book, in the early eighties, the navy had reached its nadir, and we were then utterly incompetent to fight Spain or any other power that had a navy at all. Shortly afterward we began timidly and hesitatingly to build up a fleet. It is amusing to recall the roundabout steps we took to accomplish our purpose. In the reaction after the colossal struggle of the Civil War our strongest and most capable men had thrown their whole energy into business, into moneymaking, into the development, and above all the exploitation and exhaustion at the most rapid rate possible, of our natural resources—mines, forests, soil, and rivers. These men were not weak men, but they permitted themselves to grow short-sighted and selfish; and while many of them down at the bottom possessed the fundamental virtues, including the fighting virtues, others were purely of the glorified huckster or glorified pawnbroker type—which when developed to the exclusion of everything else makes about as poor a national type as the world has seen. This unadulterated huckster or pawnbroker type is rarely keenly sympathetic in matters of social and industrial justice, and is usually physically timid and likes to cover an unworthy fear of the most just war under high-sounding names.

It was reinforced by the large mollycoddle vote—the people who are soft physically and morally, or who have a twist in them which makes them acidly cantankerous and unpleasant as long as they can be so with safety to their bodies. In addition there are the good people with no imagination and no foresight, who think war will not come, but that if it does come armies and navies can be improvised—a very large element, typified by a senator I knew personally who, in a public speech, in answer to a question as to what we would do if America were suddenly assailed by a first-class military power, answered that "we would build a battleship in every creek." Then, among the wise and high-minded people who in self-respecting and genuine fashion strive earnestly for peace, there are the foolish fanatics always to be found in such a movement and always discrediting it—the men who form the lunatic fringe in all reform movements.

All these elements taken together made a body of public opinion so important during the decades immediately succeeding the Civil War as to put a stop to any serious effort to keep the nation in a condition of reasonable military preparedness. The representatives of this opinion then voted just as they now do when they vote against battleships or against fortifying the Panama Canal. It would have been bad enough if we had been content to be weak, and, in view of our weakness, not to bluster. But we were not content with such a policy. We wished to enjoy the incompatible luxuries of an unbridled tongue and an unready hand. There was a very large element which was ignorant of our military weakness, or, naturally enough, unable to understand it; and another large element which liked to please its own vanity by listening to offensive talk about foreign nations. Accordingly, too many of our politicians, especially in Congress, found that the cheap and easy thing to do was to please the foolish peace people by keeping us weak, and to please the foolish violent people by passing denunciatory resolutions about international matters—resolutions which would have been improper even if we had been strong. Their idea was to please both the mollycoddle vote and the vote of the international tail-twisters by upholding, with pretended ardor and mean intelligence, a national policy of peace with insult.

I abhor unjust war. I abhor injustice and bullying by the strong at the expense of the weak, whether among nations or individuals. I abhor violence and bloodshed. I believe that war should never be resorted to when, or so long as, it is honorably possible to avoid it. I respect all men and women who from high motives and with sanity and self-respect do all they can to avert war. I advocate preparation for war in order to avert war; and I should never advocate war unless it were the only alternative to dishonor. I describe the folly of which so many of our people were formerly guilty, in order that we may in our own day be on our guard against similar folly.

Theodore Roosevelt, *Autobiography*. New York: Macmillan, 1913.

Document 12: The Conservation of Wildlife

Roosevelt's passion for wildlife and keen eye as an accomplished naturalist did not diminish with age. The ex-president was moved to comment on wildlife in this book review published in 1915. It is an example of Roosevelt's continued leadership on conservation issues even in retirement.

Ever since man in recognizably human shape made his appearance on this planet he has been an appreciable factor in the destruction of other forms of animal life, and he has been a potent factor ever since he developed the weapons known to the savages of the last few tens of thousands of years. But modern weapons have given a tremendous impetus to this destruction. Never before were such enormous quantities of big beasts and large birds slain as in the nineteenth century. Never before was there such extensive and wasteful slaughter of strange and beautiful forms of wild life as in the century which saw the greatest advance in material civilization and the most rapid spread of the civilized peoples throughout all the world.

Toward the end of that century a few civilized nations wakened to a sense of shame at what was going on. Enlightened men and women here and there began to take efficient action to restrain this senseless destruction of that which, once destroyed, could never be replaced. Gradually they roused a more general sentiment, and now there is a considerable body of public opinion in favor of keeping for our children's children, as a priceless heritage, all the delicate beauty of the lesser and all the burly majesty of the mightier forms of wild life. We are fast learning that trees must not be cut down more rapidly than they are replaced; we have taken forward steps in learning that wild beasts and birds are by right not the property merely of the people alive to-day, but the property of the unborn generations, whose belongings we have no right to squander; and there are even faint signs of our growing to understand that wild flowers should be enjoyed unplucked where they grow, and that it is barbarism to ravage the woods and fields, rooting out the mayflower and breaking branches of dogwood as ornaments for automobiles filled with jovial but ignorant picnickers from cities.

In the present century the new movement gathered head. Men began to appreciate the need of preserving wild life, not only because it was useful, but also because it was beautiful. Song-birds, shore-birds, water-fowl, birds of all kinds, add by voice and action to the joy of living of most men and women to whom the phrase "joy of living" has any real meaning. Such stately or lovely wild creatures as moose, wapiti, deer, hartbeest, zebra, gazelle, when protected give ample commercial returns, and, moreover, add to the landscape just as waterfalls and lofty pine-trees and towering crags add to the landscape. Fertile plains, every foot of them tilled, are of the first necessity; but great natural playgrounds of mountain, forest, cliff-walled lake, and brawling brook are also necessary to the full and many-sided development of a fine race. In just the same way the homely birds of farm and lawn and the wild creatures of the waste should all be kept. It is utterly untrue to say, as demagogues and selfish materialists sometimes unite in saying, that "the game belongs to the people"—meaning the loafers and market gunners who wish to kill it, and the wealthy and lazy gourmands who wish to eat it, without regard to the future. It is true that the game belongs to the people; but this rightly means the people who are to be born a hundred years hence just as much as the people who are alive to-day. In the same way, persons who own land, and, above all, persons who merely visit or pass through land, have no more right wantonly or carelessly to destroy birds or deface scenery than they have to pollute waters or burn down forests or let floods through levees. The sooner we appreciate these facts, the sooner we shall become a really civilized people.

Laws to protect small and harmless wild life, especially birds, are indispensable. Such laws cannot be enacted or enforced until public opinion is in back of them; and associations like the Audubon Societies do work of incalculable good in stirring, rousing, and giving effect to this opinion; and men like Mr. [William T.] Hornaday [author of *Wild Life Conservation*] render all of us their debtors by the way they efficiently labor for this end, as well as for what comes only next in importance, the creation of sanctuaries for the complete protection of the larger, shyer, and more persecuted forms of wild life. This country led the way in establishing the Yellowstone Park as such a sanctuary; the British and German Empires followed, and in many ways have surpassed us. There are now many such sanctuaries and refuges in North America, middle and South Africa, and even Asia, and the results have been astounding. Many of the finer forms of animal life, which seemed on the point of vanishing, are now far more numerous than fifteen years ago, having by their rapid increase given proof of the abounding vigor of nature's fertility where nature is unmarred by man. But very much remains to be done, and there is need of the most active warfare against the forces of greed, carelessness, and sheer brutality, which, if left unchecked, would speedily undo all that has been accomplished, and would inflict literally irreparable damage.

Theodore Roosevelt, *The Outlook*, January 20, 1915; reprinted in Mario R. DiNunzio, *Theodore Roosevelt: An American Mind: Selected Writings.* New York: Penguin, 1994, pp. 291–97.

Document 13: Remarks on Presenting the Medal of Honor

Theodore Roosevelt showed such bravery during the course of the battle for San Juan Hill on July 1, 1898, that he was recommended for the Medal of Honor. For political reasons, he was denied the award. However, as testimony to his enduring courage, just over a century later he received the award posthumously in these comments by President Bill Clinton in 2001.

In 1782 George Washington created the Badge of Military Merit. It was the first medal awarded by our Nation's Armed Forces. But soon it fell into oblivion, and for decades no new medals were established. It was thought that a medal was too much like a European aristocratic title, while to fight for one's country in America was simply doing your democratic duty.

So when the Medal of Honor was instituted during the Civil War, it was agreed it would be given only for gallantry, at the risk of one's life above and beyond the call of duty. That's an extraordinarily high standard, one that precious few ever meet. The Medal of Honor is our highest military decoration, and we are here today to honor two American heroes who met that mark. . . .

The second Medal of Honor I award today is for the bravery of Lieutenant Colonel Theodore Roosevelt on July 1, 1898. That was the day he led his volunteer troops, the Rough Riders, in taking San Juan Hill, which changed the course of the battle and the Spanish-American War.

We are greatly honored to be joined today by members of the Roosevelt family, including Tweed Roosevelt, here to accept the Medal of Honor on behalf of his great-grandfather.

This is the 37th Medal of Honor I have presented, but the first I presented in the recipient's old office in front of a portrait of him in full battle gear. It is a tradition in the Roosevelt Room that when a Democrat is in the White House, a portrait of Franklin Roosevelt hangs above the mantle, and when a Republican is here, Teddy Roosevelt occupies the hallowed spot. I chose to break with the tradition these last

8 years because I figured if we could have even half the luck and skill leading America into the 21st century that Theodore Roosevelt did in leading America into the 20th century, our Nation would do just fine.

TR was a larger-than-life figure who gave our Nation a larger-than-life vision of our place in the world. Part of that vision was formed on San Juan Hill. His Rough Riders were made up of all kinds of Americans from all walks of life. They were considered unpolished and undisciplined, but they were true citizen soldiers. By taking San Juan Hill, eventually they forced the enemy fleet into the Battle of Santiago Bay, where it was routed. This led to the Spanish surrender and opened the era of America as a global power.

Twenty-two people won the Medal of Honor for actions that day. Two high-ranking military officers who had won the Medal of Honor in earlier wars and who saw Theodore Roosevelt's bravery recommended him for the medal, too. For some reason, the War Department never acted on the recommendation. Some say he didn't get it because of the bias the War Department had against volunteers. Others say it was because he ran afoul of the Secretary of War, who, after the war, was reluctant to allow the return of a number of American servicemen afflicted with yellow fever. Roosevelt publicly called for America to bring its heroes home, where they had a far better chance to recover. The administration had to reverse course, and it proved embarrassing to the Secretary.

But while opinions about why he didn't receive the medal are mixed, opinion that he should have received it long ago is unanimous. So here in this room will stand two great bookends to his wide-ranging life: the Medal of Honor, America's highest honor for warriors; and the Nobel Peace Prize, the world's highest honor for peacemakers, which he won for his role in settling the Russo-Japanese War of 1905.

This is a remarkable day, and I can't help but noting that for historical buffs, Theodore Roosevelt's son was the oldest man who landed on the beaches at Normandy on D-day, where he also won the Medal of Honor. Tragically, he died shortly after that, in his uniform doing his duty.

We are profoundly grateful as Americans for this remarkable family. And I am honored that I had the chance before I left office to correct what I think is a significant historical error.

Bill Clinton, excerpts from the posthumous awarding of the Medal of Honor to Theodore Roosevelt, January 16, 2001.

CHRONOLOGY

OCTOBER 27, 1858
Theodore Roosevelt is born at 28 East 20th Street in New York City.

MAY 12, 1869
Roosevelt embarks on a tour of Europe with his family.

1876–1880
Roosevelt attends Harvard University; he graduates magna cum laude, twenty-first in a class of 177.

FEBRUARY 9, 1878
Theodore Roosevelt Sr., Teddy's father, dies.

1880–1882
Roosevelt attends Columbia Law School but drops out before graduating.

OCTOBER 27, 1880
Roosevelt marries Alice Hathaway Lee.

NOVEMBER 8, 1881
Roosevelt is elected to the New York State Assembly; he serves three 1-year terms.

1882
Roosevelt's first book *The Naval War of 1812* is published; he joins the New York National Guard.

1883
Roosevelt is elected the minority leader in the Assembly; he establishes two ranches in the Dakota Territory.

1884–1885
Roosevelt lives in the Dakota Territory, writing, hunting, and working as a rancher.

FEBRUARY 12, 1884
Daughter Alice Lee Roosevelt is born.

FEBRUARY 14, 1884
On the same day, Roosevelt's mother dies of typhoid and his wife, Alice, dies of a kidney infection.

1885
Roosevelt's book *Hunting Trips of a Ranchman* is published.

NOVEMBER 17, 1885
Roosevelt becomes engaged to Edith Kermit Carrow.

NOVEMBER 4, 1886
Roosevelt is defeated in the mayoral election of New York City.

DECEMBER 2, 1886
Roosevelt marries Edith in London.

SEPTEMBER 13, 1887
Son Theodore Jr. is born.

1888
Roosevelt's books *Life of Gouverneur Morris, Ranch Life and the Hunting Trail,* and *Essays on Practical Politics* are published.

1889
Roosevelt is appointed civil service commissioner for the federal government and serves until 1895; the first two volumes of the four-volume set *The Winning of the West* are published.

OCTOBER 10, 1889
Son Kermit is born.

1891
History of New York is published.

AUGUST 13, 1891
Daughter Ethel is born.

1893
The Wilderness Hunter is published.

1894
The third volume of *The Winning of the West* is published.

APRIL 10, 1894
Son Archibald is born.

1895
Hero Tales from American History is published.

MAY 5, 1895
Roosevelt resigns as civil service commissioner to become police commissioner of New York City; he initiates a variety of reforms within the department, winning him national attention.

1896
The fourth and final volume of *The Winning of the West* is published.

1897
American Ideals is published.

APRIL 19, 1897
President William McKinley appoints Roosevelt the assistant secretary of the navy.

JUNE 2, 1897
Roosevelt's speech at the Naval War College in Newport, Rhode Island, attracts national attention.

NOVEMBER 19, 1897
Son Quentin is born.

APRIL 19, 1898
The United States declares war on Spain.

May 6, 1898

Roosevelt receives commission as a lieutenant colonel in a volunteer cavalry unit known as the "Rough Riders."

July 1, 1898

Roosevelt leads the Rough Riders in the Battle of San Juan Hill and is nominated for the Medal of Honor (which was denied) and promoted to colonel.

October 5, 1898

Roosevelt delivers the famous speech "Duties of a Great Nation" at the opening of Carnegie Hall.

November 8, 1898

Roosevelt is elected governor of New York; once in office, he supports a variety of reform measures.

1899

The Rough Riders is published.

November 6, 1900

Incumbent president William McKinley, with Roosevelt as his vice presidential candidate, wins election.

March 4, 1901

Roosevelt is inaugurated as vice president.

September 6, 1901

President McKinley is shot in an assassination attempt by Leon Czolgosz; the president dies on September 13 and Roosevelt is sworn in as president the next day.

October 16, 1901

Roosevelt invites well-known black leader Booker T. Washington to dinner at the White House.

February 19, 1902

Roosevelt orders an antitrust investigation of Northern Securities under the Sherman Anti-Trust Act, the first of forty-five such actions against trusts and monopolies.

MAY 22, 1902

Crater Lake National Park is established, the first of five parks established by Roosevelt.

JUNE 17, 1902

Roosevelt signs the Newlands Reclamation Act, one of twenty-four federal irrigation projects enacted while he is president.

JUNE 28, 1902

Congress authorizes Roosevelt to negotiate a treaty to construct a canal through Panama.

SEPTEMBER 3, 1902

Roosevelt is injured in a trolley accident.

OCTOBER 17, 1902

Roosevelt arbitrates and settles the Anthracite Coal Strike.

FEBRUARY 14, 1903

The Department of Commerce and Labor is established.

MARCH 14, 1903

Roosevelt establishes Pelican Island, Florida, as the first federal bird reservation; he eventually approves a total of fifty-one such reservations.

OCTOBER 22, 1903

Roosevelt appoints the Public Lands Commission to examine land policy; it is the first of seven commissions or major conferences on the environment convened by Roosevelt.

NOVEMBER 1903

Roosevelt authorizes the use of military force to support the Panamanian Revolution in order to ensure that the United States has the ability to construct a canal across the isthmus; a treaty between the United States and Panama authorizing the canal is signed on November 18.

NOVEMBER 8, 1904
Roosevelt is elected for a second term (but his first election as the presidential candidate).

DECEMBER 6, 1904
Roosevelt issues the "Roosevelt Corollary" to the Monroe Doctrine, which authorizes American military interventions in order to forestall European interference in the Western Hemisphere.

1905
Outdoor Pastimes of an American Hunter is published.

FEBRUARY 1, 1905
Roosevelt creates the National Forest Service.

MARCH 4, 1905
Roosevelt is inaugurated as president.

MARCH 17, 1905
Roosevelt stands in for his deceased brother, Elliot, during niece Eleanor Roosevelt's wedding to Franklin D. Roosevelt, who would become president in 1933.

JUNE 2, 1905
The first federal game preserve at Wichita Forest, Oklahoma, is established; three others follow, including the Grand Canyon in 1908.

SEPTEMBER 5, 1905
Roosevelt mediates the Russo-Japanese War by negotiating the Treaty of Portsmouth.

JANUARY 1906
To prevent the outbreak of conflict between France and Germany over influence in Morocco, Roosevelt mediates a resolution that is acceptable to all parties.

JUNE 8, 1906

Roosevelt signs the National Monuments Act and ultimately creates eighteen national monuments, including Devils Tower, the Petrified Forest, and Mount Olympus.

JUNE 29, 1906

Roosevelt signs the Hepburn Act, which creates the Interstate Commerce Commission; the next day, he signs the Pure Food and Drug Act.

NOVEMBER 8–26, 1906

Roosevelt and Edith travel to inspect progress on the Panama Canal and become the first president and first lady to travel outside of the United States while in office.

DECEMBER 10, 1906

Roosevelt is awarded the Nobel Peace Prize for his efforts to end the Russo-Japanese War.

NOVEMBER 19, 1907

Roosevelt informs his cabinet that in keeping with tradition, he will not seek another term as president.

DECEMBER 16, 1907

Roosevelt orders the "Great White Fleet" to circumnavigate the globe to demonstrate the naval power of the United States.

MAY 13, 1908

Roosevelt convenes a conference on the conservation of natural resources.

JULY 22, 1908

Roosevelt delivers the address "Why the Nation Needs an Effective Navy" at the Naval War College.

FEBRUARY 22, 1909

The Great White Fleet returns after a sixteen-month voyage.

MARCH 4, 1909

Roosevelt leaves office after the inauguration of his hand-picked successor, William Howard Taft.

MARCH 23, 1909

Roosevelt embarks on an African safari (during which he gathers specimens for the Smithsonian Institution), followed by a tour of Europe (he returns to the United States in June of the following year).

1910

African Game Trails is published.

APRIL 23, 1910

Roosevelt delivers his famous speech "Citizenship in a Republic" at the Sorbonne in France.

FEBRUARY 21, 1911

Roosevelt announces his candidacy for the presidency in the 1912 election.

1912

Realizable Ideals is published.

JUNE 1912

Taft secures the Republican nomination after party conservatives refuse to seat Roosevelt's delegates to the convention.

AUGUST 1912

Roosevelt accepts the presidential nomination of the Progressive Party.

OCTOBER 14, 1912

While campaigning in Milwaukee, Wisconsin, Roosevelt is shot by John F. Schrank; he goes on to deliver a ninety-minute speech before going to the hospital.

NOVEMBER 5, 1912

Woodrow Wilson wins the presidential election; Roosevelt comes in second and Taft third.

1913

Theodore Roosevelt: An Autobiography and *History as Literature and Other Essays* are published.

OCTOBER 4, 1913

Roosevelt and his son Kermit depart on a six-month-long South American tour and jungle exploration sponsored by the American Museum of Natural History.

1914

World War I begins; *Through the Brazilian Wilderness* and *Life Histories of African Game Animals* are published.

1915

America and the World War is published.

1916

A Book Lover's Holidays in the Open and *Fear God and Take Your Own Park* are published.

JUNE 10, 1916

The Progressive Party again tries to nominate Roosevelt for president, but he declines.

1917

Foes of Our Household is published.

FEBRUARY 1917

Roosevelt requests permission to lead an infantry division in the war; the request is denied by the Wilson administration; however, all of Roosevelt's sons enlist to serve in the military and his daughter Ethel serves as a nurse in the Red Cross.

JULY 14, 1917

Roosevelt's son Quentin is shot down and killed while serving as a fighter pilot in France.

1918

The Great Adventure is published.

JULY 1918

Roosevelt refuses the Republican nomination for the governorship of New York.

JANUARY 6, 1919

Roosevelt dies in his sleep of a coronary embolism.

JANUARY 2001

Posthumously receives Medal of Honor (nominated in 1898) from President Bill Clinton for valor in the Battle of San Juan Hill in the Spanish-American War.

FOR FURTHER RESEARCH

GENERAL BIOGRAPHY AND LIFE

H.W. BRANDS, *TR: The Last Romantic*. New York: BasicBooks, 1997.

DAVID HENRY BURTON, *Theodore Roosevelt*. New York: Twayne, 1972.

G. WALLACE CHESSMAN, *Theodore Roosevelt and the Politics of Power*. Boston: Little, Brown, 1969.

NATHAN MILLER, *Theodore Roosevelt: A Life*. New York: William Morrow, 1994.

EDMUND MORRIS, *Theodore Rex*, New York: Random House, 2001.

HENRY F. PRINGLE, *Theodore Roosevelt: A Biography*. New York: Harcourt, Brace, 1931.

THEODORE ROOSEVELT, *Theodore Roosevelt: An Autobiography*. 1913. Reprint, New York: Da Capo, 1985.

EARLY LIFE AND CAREER

H. PAUL JEFFERS, *Colonel Roosevelt: Theodore Roosevelt Goes to War, 1897–1898*. New York: John Wiley, 1996.

———, *Commissioner Roosevelt: The Story of Theodore Roosevelt and the New York City Police, 1895–1897*. New York: John Wiley, 1996.

DAVID MCCULLOGH, *Mornings on Horseback: The Story of an Extraordinary Family, a Vanished Way of Life, and the Unique Child Who Became Theodore Roosevelt*. New York: Simon and Schuster, 1981.

EDMUND MORRIS, *The Rise of Theodore Roosevelt*. New York: Coward, McCann & Geoghegan, 1979.

CARLETON PUTNAM, *Theodore Roosevelt: The Formative Years, 1858–1886*. New York: Charles Scribner's Sons, 1958.

PEGGY SAMUELS AND HAROLD SAMUELS, *Teddy Roosevelt at San Juan: The Making of a President*. College Station: Texas A&M University Press, 1997.

DALE L. WALKER, *The Boys of '98: Theodore Roosevelt and the Rough Riders*. Thousand Oaks, CA: Forge, 1999.

ROOSEVELT'S FAMILY

CAROL FELSENTHAL, *Princess Alice: The Life and Times of Alice Roosevelt Longworth*. New York: St. Martin's, 1988.

TOM LANSFORD, *A "Bully" First Lady: Edith Kermit Roosevelt*. Huntington, NY: Nova History Publications, 2001.

SYLVIA JUKES MORRIS, *Edith Kermit Roosevelt: Portrait of a First Lady*. New York: Modern Library, 2001.

EDWARD J. RENEHAN JR., *The Lion's Pride: Theodore Roosevelt and His Family in Peace and War*. Washington, DC: Getty Center for Education in the Arts, 1994.

CORINNE ROOSEVELT ROBINSON, *My Brother Theodore Roosevelt*. New York: Charles Scribner's Sons, 1921.

DOROTHY CLARKE WILSON, *Alice and Edith: The Two Wives of Theodore Roosevelt: A Biographical Novel*. New York: Doubleday, 1989.

CONSERVATION AND DOMESTIC POLICY

JOHN MORTON BLUM, *The Republican Roosevelt*. Cambridge, MA: Harvard University Press, 1954.

PAUL RUSSELL CUTRIGHT, *Theodore Roosevelt: The Making of a Conservationist*. Urbana: University of Illinois Press, 1985.

———, *Theodore Roosevelt the Naturalist*. New York: Harper, 1956.

LEWIS L. GOULD, *The Presidency of Theodore Roosevelt*. Lawrence: University of Kansas Press, 1991.

INTERNATIONAL AFFAIRS AND THE PANAMA CANAL

DAVID H. BURTON, *Theodore Roosevelt: Confident Imperialist.* Philadelphia: University of Pennsylvania Press, 1968.

RICHARD H. COLLINS, *Theodore Roosevelt: Culture, Diplomacy, and Expansion.* Baton Rouge: Louisiana State University Press, 1985.

———, *Theodore Roosevelt's Caribbean: The Panama Canal, the Monroe Doctrine, and the Latin American Context.* Baton Rouge: Louisiana State University Press, 1990.

WALTER LAFEBER, *The Panama Canal: The Crisis in Historical Perspective.* New York: Oxford University Press, 1978.

DAVID McCULLOUGH, *The Path Between the Seas: The Creation of the Panama Canal, 1870–1914.* 2nd ed. New York: Simon and Schuster, 1999.

ROOSEVELT'S NAVY AND MILITARY POLICY

HOWARD K. BEALE, *Theodore Roosevelt and the Rise of America to World Power.* Baltimore: Johns Hopkins University Press, 1956.

FREDERICK W. MARKS III, *Velvet on Iron: The Diplomacy of Theodore Roosevelt.* Lincoln: University of Nebraska Press, 1979.

EDWARD J. MAROLDA, ED., *Theodore Roosevelt, the U.S. Navy, and the Spanish-American War.* New York: Palgrave, 2001.

JAMES R. RECKNER, *Teddy Roosevelt's Great White Fleet.* Annapolis: Naval Institute Press, 1988.

RICHARD W. TURK, *The Ambiguous Relationship: Theodore Roosevelt and Alfred Thayer Mahan.* Westport, CT: Greenwood, 1987.

LETTERS AND POSTPRESIDENTIAL YEARS

JOSEPH BUCKLIN BISHOP, ED., *Theodore Roosevelt and His Time, Shown in His Letters.* 2 vols. New York: Charles Scribner's Sons, 1920.

H.W. BRANDS, ED., *The Selected Letters of Theodore Roosevelt.* New York: Cooper Square, 2001.

MARIO R. DINUNZIO, *Theodore Roosevelt, an American Mind: A Selection from His Writings.* New York: Penguin, 1995.

JOSEPH LAWRENCE GARDNER, *Departing Glory: Theodore Roosevelt as Ex-President.* New York: Charles Scribner's Sons, 1973.

JOHN GABRIEL HUNT, ED., *The Essential Theodore Roosevelt.* New York: Gramercy, 1998.

ELTING MORISON AND JOHN M. BLUM ET AL., EDS., *The Letters of Theodore Roosevelt.* 8 vols. Cambridge, MA: Harvard University Press, 1951–1954.

THEODORE ROOSEVELT, *Theodore Roosevelt's Letters to His Children.* New York: Norwood Editions, 1919.

FREDERICK W. WOOD, ED., *Roosevelt as We Knew Him: The Personal Recollections of One Hundred and Fifty of His Friends and Associates.* Philadelphia: John C. Winston, 1927.

Index

Hay, John, 21, 120, 122, 136, 156
  negotiations with Colombia
    by, 145–46
Hay-Bunau-Varilla Treaty, 21
Hay-Herrán Convention, 146
Hay-Herrán Treaty, 139
Hay-Pauncefote agreement, 143
Hays, Samuel P., 55
Hepburn Act of 1906, 24, 100
Herran, Tomas, 145
Hill, James J., 63, 88, 104
Hoar, George F., 91
Hobart, Garret, 18
Hofstadter, Richard, 100, 101,
  130
Howard-Pitney, David, 59
Howland, Harold, 44, 79
Hunting Trips of a Ranchman
  (Theodore Roosevelt), 34

*Influence of Sea Power Upon
  History, 1669–1783* (Mahan),
  25, 155
Inland Waterways Commission,
  42, 60, 61
internationalism, American
  Roosevelt as father of, 112–18
Interstate Commerce
  Commission
  creation of, 24
irrigation projects, 40, 46–47

Jackson, Andrew, 128
Japan
  rise as naval power, 26
  violation of "open door" policy
    by, 121
Jefferson, Thomas, 55, 177
Johnson, Arthur M., 83, 99
Jungle, The (Sinclair), 164

Kermit, Edith, 15
Key, Albert L., 171, 172
Kissinger, Henry, 113
Knight case, 84
Knox, Philander C., 87, 90, 93
Kolko, Gabriel, 100

labor
  Roosevelt increased
    government involvement in,
    87–97
Lafeber, Walter, 119
League of Nations, 114
Lee, Alice Hathaway, 13
  death of, 13
Letwin, William, 99
Lewis and Clark expedition, 55
Lincoln, Abraham, 128, 177
Literary Digest (magazine), 88
Lodge, Henry Cabot, 92, 93, 155,
  156
Loeb, William, 93, 169
Long, John D., 155, 165, 169
Loomis, F.B., 147
Lucas, Stephen, 99

Madison, James, 120, 121
Mahan, Alfred Thayer, 25,
  117–18, 127, 155, 182
  big-gun battleships and,
    179–80
Maine (U.S. battleship)
  sinking of the, 16
Markle, John B., 94
Marks, Frederick W., III, 130
Marroquín, Jose M., 133, 136,
  146
Marvinney, Sandy, 32
McClure's Magazine, 184
McConnell, Grant, 100
McGowan, Samuel, 167, 168

ABOUT THE EDITORS

Tom Lansford, Ph.D., and Robert P. Watson, Ph.D., are on the editorial board of the journal *White House Studies*. Tom Lansford is assistant professor of political science at the University of Southern Mississippi. Among his many book credits are *The Lords of Foggy Bottom: The American Secretaries of State and the World They Shaped* (2001) and *A Bully First Lady: Edith Roosevelt* (2001). Robert P. Watson, the founding editor of *White House Studies*, is a visiting associate professor of political science at Florida Atlantic University. He is the author or editor of twelve books and more than 100 scholarly articles and essays on American politics, the presidency, first ladies, public policy, and civil rights.